Y0-ATA-639

SINO-RUSSIAN RELATIONS
IN THE SEVENTEENTH CENTURY

SINO-RUSSIAN RELATIONS
IN THE
SEVENTEENTH CENTURY

by

VINCENT CHEN

St. John's University

MARTINUS NIJHOFF / THE HAGUE / 1966

Copyright 1966 by Martinus Nijhoff, The Hague, Netherlands.
All rights reserved, including the right to translate or to
reproduce this book or parts thereof in any form.

LIBRARY
FLORIDA STATE UNIVERSITY
TALLAHASSEE, FLORIDA

PRINTED IN THE NETHERLANDS

TO
ELLEN

ACKNOWLEDGMENT

Acknowledgment is hereby made for the materials of various sources which the author has used for the preparation of this book, especially for the permissions granted by Macmillan & Co., Ltd., London, to quote from John P. Baddeley (ed.), *Russia, Mongolia, China*, and by Rev. Joseph S. Sebes, S.J., to quote from his book *The Jesuits and the Sino-Russian Treaty of Nerchinsk (1689)*, and for the quotations translated from Chinese by Miss Agnes Fang-chih Chen in her article "Chinese Frontier Diplomacy: (1) The Coming of the Russians and the Treaty of Nerchinsk; (2) Kiakhta Boundary Treaties and Agreements;" *The Yenching Journal of Social Studies*, IV (February, 1949). The author wishes to express a special indebtedness to Professor Earl H. Pritchard for his critical reading of the manuscript and valuable advice and suggestions.

CONTENTS

INTRODUCTION

The seventeenth century was a momentous epoch. While western European countries were busy expanding westward and eastward, Russia, quietly crossed the Ural Mountains, absorbed Siberia and reached as far as Alaska. Russia did not expand toward the East without opposition from the western European countries. In the last half of the sixteenth century, inspired by the "gorgeous East," the Dutch and the English made many efforts to find a northern passage to China to attain gold, gems, silks, pearls and spices.[1] They attempted to reach China by land routes but were hindered by continual wars between the Kazaks and Mongol tribes, as is indicated in a letter written by an English traveler, Jenkinson, in 1559.[2] They also attempted to reach China by way of the Northern Ocean, but the Arctic weather foiled all of these efforts.

The English hoped to find a way to China as well as to India by the Ob River. They knew of the Ob as early as 1555, and the next year Stephen Burrough was sent to find it. He reached the Kara Strait but ice prevented him from passing through it. In 1580 Arthur Pet and Charles Jackman left England with two ships in search of a northeast passage. Pet went through the Kara Strait. Jackman followed him in 1581, encountering much ice. Eventually Pet's expedition succeeded in returning westward again through the Kara Strait, but Jackman and his men were never heard from again. Jackman's instructions had been to sail up the Ob and, if possible, to reach the city of Sibir. They might have reached the Ob during the heat of the contest between Yermak and Kuchum, which will be considered later. The Siberian chieftain Mametkul, nephew of the Kuchum Khan, captured in 1583 by Yermak, told of some Englishmen in his country, who had been

---

[1] John F. Baddeley, *Russia, Mongolia, China* (London: Macmillan & Co., 1919), I, lxxxix.
[2] *Ibid.*, I, lxvii.

taken prisoner together with a ship, ordnance, powder and other riches; however, this was two years before Jackman's party could have passed the Ob to seek China by the North Sea. It seems probable that Jackman and his men were mistaken for Russians or their allies and were killed by the Kuchums.[1]

In 1594–1597 Dutch ships, some under Nai and Linschoten, sailed eastward through Yugor Straits, while others under Barentsz, rounding Nova Zembla, but all were baffled in the dreaded "Cronian" sea as shown in the picture:[2]

> Mountains of ice, that stop th'imagin'd way
> Beyond 'Petsora' Eastward, to the
> rich 'Cathaian' Coast:

The Barentsz expedition was abandoned on that barren shore, in lat. 76° 7′ N., where its gallant commander died of scurvy, leaving his crew to an adventurous escape in a makeshift boat.

After this failure the English and Dutch turned their efforts to reach China to warm seas. However, the English did not give up their interest in reaching China by the Ob. The English envoy to Russia, Mericke, having helped to bring about the Stolbovski treaty of peace between Sweden and Russia in 1617, asked in reward certain privileges for English commerce from Russia, particularly permission for English merchants to go by the Volga to Persia, and also to seek a way by the Ob to India and China. Russia refused the English request on the grounds of the cold weather of Siberia, the impossibility of navigation of the Ob and the absence of authentic information about China and Siberia. As to China, the Russian boyars told the English envoy that it was completely surrounded by a brick wall, the Great Wall, from which it was evident that it was no large place. The English attempts were thus frustrated by the Russians, and Russia was left free to exploit northern Asia by land and monopolize trade with eastern countries by the overland route.[3]

This eastward expansion contributed to Russia's growing power which enabled her to play an increasingly important role as a world power in later days. Therefore, the expansion of Russia in northern Asia and her relations with China in the seventeenth century should be of interest to historians as well as to statesmen and political scientists. Nevertheless, there are few works dealing with early Sino-Russian

---

[1] *Ibid.*, II, 66–67.
[2] *Ibid.*, I, lxxxix, quoting *Paradise Lost*, Bk. X, ll. 290–293.
[3] *Ibid.*, II, 66.

relations and most of them start with the Treaty of Nerchinsk. Several collections of documents and related materials pertain to the seventeenth century, but they do not give us a clear picture of the relations between Russia and China.

In taking up the subject of Sino-Russian relations in the seventeenth century, the writer relies on both Chinese and Russian sources, of which two books, Ho Chiu-tao's *So-fang pei-ch'eng* and John P. Baddeley's *Russia, Mongolia, China* are of prime importance. The former is a collection of material from various Chinese sources providing historical and geographical descriptions of northern Asia from very early times up to 1858. The collection was compiled and edited by Ho Chiu-tao, an authority on history and geography. It consists of eighty *chüan* (sections) of which twenty-two relate directly to the period of the seventeenth century. No date of publication is given, but the work was finished and presented to the Hsien-feng Emperor in 1858. Later the book was lost in loose pages, and Viceroy Li Hung-chang ordered a scholar named Huang Peng-nien to recompile the collection on the basis of the original manuscript. After the recompilation was accomplished, Li himself wrote a preface to the book and recommended it to the public on its merits. The collection consists of edicts, memoirs, biographies, strategic plans, extracts from official history and various books approved by the Chinese Emperors as well as many monographs written by Chinese like Chang Mu, Wei Yüan, and Tu Li-shen, by Jesuits such as Ferdinand Verbiest (Nan Hua-jen) and Jules Aleni (Yen Ju-lüeh), and by other westerners. By comparing these official and private sources, Ho rectified errors found in the record.

Russia, Mongolia, China is a record of the relations between the three countries from the beginning of the seventeenth century to the death of the Csar Alexei Mikhailovich in 1676. It consists mainly of narratives dictated or written by the envoys sent by the Russian Csars, or their *voevodas* in Siberia, to the Kalmuk and Mongol Khans and princes, and to the Emperors of China. To the main body of the material were added historical and geographical introductions and a series of maps showing the progress of geographical knowledge in regard to northern Asia during the sixteenth, seventeenth and early eighteenth centuries. The texts were taken especially from manuscripts in the Archives of the Moscow foreign office. The whole work was compiled and translated from Russian into English by John J. Baddeley, who had travelled in Russia and most parts of northern Asia for the purpose of study and who is an authority on the history and geography of Russia, Siberia, Turkestan, Mongolia and China. These two main sources, the Chinese *So-fang pei-ch'eng* and the Russian *Russia, Mongolia, China*, are very reliable. Naturally, divergent points of view are revealed in the two collections. The writer, however, tries to reach a fair conclusion by weighing and checking both the Chinese and Russian materials.

This treatise attempts to present a concise and systematic account of Sino-Russian relations in the seventeenth century. The treatment of the subject will emphasize the power relationship between the two empires in terms of their geographical conditions, historical backgrounds, social settings, political leadership and other internal and external relationships. Since Mongol tribes lay between the two empires, the Russians had to cross their lands when coming to China, and the Mongols played an important role in the relationship between the two empires. Thus the relations between Russia, Mongolia and China have to be explored to a certain extent. To the writer it seemes most convenient to present certain phases of the subject as general topics which cover the whole century, while in other cases the material is best handled on a rather strict chronological basis.[1] Thus the chapter "Geographical and Historical Descriptions of Northern Asia" traces back earlier events, stressing some influential elements in earlier political development. The chapters on the "Expansions of Russia and China in Northern Asia" and "The Role of the Mongols in Sino-Russian Relations," embrace the events of the whole century. These three chapters serve to lay down the general background for the latter treatment. Then follow three chapters which deal with Russia's attempts to establish diplomatic relations with China or to colonize the Amur; they proceed chronologically. Among them, Spathary's mission will be treated fully so as to illustrate how the Chinese court received the Russian envoys in early times. "Sino-Russian War on the Amur" and "The Treaty of Nerchinsk" climaxed the prominant events in the seventeenth century. As a result of these contacts, commercial and cultural relations developed steadily. It is necessary to have one separate chapter for them in view of their significance.

---

[1] All Chinese dates are translated into the western calender, with the help of Hsüeh and Ouyang's *A Sino-Western Calender for Two Thousand Years*, Liu's *A Table of the Chinese Calender of Fifty Centuries*, and Ti's *A Calender Table of Leading Events of the World*.

CHAPTER II

GEOGRAPHICAL AND HISTORICAL DESCRIPTIONS OF NORTHERN ASIA

I. GEOGRAPHICAL CONDITIONS

Northern Asia as used in this treatise comprises Siberia, Turkestan, Mongolia and Manchuria, and amounts to almost one-half of the whole continent of Asia, although its population is only a fraction of Asia's total.[1]

Siberia may be regarded as consisting of two parts: (1) Western Siberia, which extends from the Ural Mountains to the River Yenisei and is flat and bounded by mountains on the south; (2) Eastern Siberia, which lies east of the Yenisei and rises gradually into hilly regions difficult of access, culminating in high mountains in the extreme east.[2] Manchuria, including the Amur region, with the Khingan Mountains on the north and west, slopes eastward to the Pacific. Its chief river is the Amur, a stream which, with its greater tributaries, affords splendid facilities for navigation. Mongolia, including inner and outer Mongolia, is a plateau with deserts in the south and higher mountain valleys in the north. Turkestan, including Sinkiang and the Kazaks region, features deserts bordering Siberia. Towering mountains, the Hindu Kush, Pamir, Tien Shan and Altai form watersheds, whence rivers fall into inland lakes and lose themselves in the desert, to reappear as oases and basins. Northern Asia as a whole has free access to the Eurasian plain in the west, but in the south it is limited to a few gateways. The plain itself is divided into two distinct zones: the forest zone in the north and the steppe zone in the south.[3]

Being shut in by mountains and deserts which keep off the moisture

---

[1] Prince A. Lobanov-Rostovsky, *Russia and Asia* (New York: The Macmillan Company, 1933), p. 2.

[2] M. A. Czaplicka, *Aboriginal Siberia* (Oxford: At the Clarendon Press, 1914), p. 3.

[3] Lobanov-Rostovsky, *op. cit.*, p. 2.

laden wind from the south, and being open to the northern winds, northern Asia, due to its great land-mass, has, generally speaking, a continental climate characterized by extremes of heat, cold and dryness. Northern Siberia can be technically termed Arctic climate, with a short warm season, low temperature and continuous light during summer, and dry winds in winter. Southern Siberia is much milder; it may be called sub-Arctic, and the characteristics of the continental climate develop gradually from north to south. It is difficult to draw a definite line between the Arctic, sub-Arctic and continental climate zones, but it may be said that low temperature conditions are found farther south in the east than in the west.[1]

The mountains of northern Asia do not form a continuous chain but rather a series of detached ranges, in the following order from the west to east: the Ural Mountains on the western border of Siberia, the Hindu Kush, Pamir and the Tien Shan ranges on the south of Russian Turkestan, the Sayan Mountains between Siberia and the plateau of Mongolia, the Altai Mountains between Turkestan and Mongolia, the Yablonoi Mountains (or Stanovoi in the northeast) between Siberia and Mongolia, and the Greater Khingan Mountains between Manchuria and Mongolia. The mountains in southern Siberia give birth to three great river systems: the Ob, having its source among the lakes and glaciers of the Altai Mountains, the Yenesei, originating from the Sayan Mountains and Lake Baikal into which the River Selenga falls from Mongolia, and the Lena, taking its rise in the Yablonoi Mountains. All the three rivers run into the Arctic Ocean.[2] In Turkestan, from the Hindu Kush and the Pamir, the Amu Darya and the Syr Darya run parallel and fall into the Aral Sea; from the Tien Shan ranges, the Ili runs into Lake Balkash.[3] Farther east in Manchuria, the Amur flows from the Yablonoi, Stanovoi and Khingan Mountains into the Pacific Ocean.[4] On the rivers are situated cities, such as Tobolsk, Omsk, Tomsk and Sibir on the tributaries of the Ob; Bukhara and Samarkand in the valley of the Amu and Syr Daryas; Ining on the Ili; Irkutsk on the Angara, a tributary on the Yenesei; Urga on a tributary of the Selenga; and Nerchinsk, Albazin and Tsitsihar on tributaries of the Amur or on the Amur itself.[5]

[1] Czaplicka, *op. cit.*, pp. 3–9.
[2] *Ibid.*, pp. 9–10.
[3] Lobanov-Rostovsky, *op. cit.*, p. 149.
[4] Czaplicka, *op. cit.*, p. 10.
[5] *Rand McNally World Atlas* (Chicago: Rand McNally & Co., 1950), p. 10. Robert J. Kerner, *The Urge to Sea* (Berkeley & Los Angeles: University of California Press, 1942), pp. 5–11.

These mountains are all well forested and rich in minerals. The valleys of the south are very fertile and well adapted to agriculture, especially in Manchuria and the southwestern Siberia. In the south, Siberia, Mongolia and Turkestan, the broad steppes and oases afford excellent ground for cattle-breeding, and a few small valleys are good for agriculture. The rivers contain plenty of excellent fish. The mountains and forests shelter various kinds of valuable animals, and furs were a resource which lured Russia to invade Siberia.[1]

In dealing with the peoples of northern Asia, we are confronted with a task of peculiar difficulty. Tribes are so various that one can hardly determine which tribe belongs to which race. For convenience of treatment, we attempt to group the peoples of the area, based on geographical and historical data, into four major groups, namely, Turks, Mongols, Tungus and Chinese. As regards the Turks, only the central and eastern groups of the Turkic race live in the area. The central group, to which Kirgis-Kazak, Kara-Kirgis, Uzebeg, Sartes, and Tartars of the Volga belong, inhabit Turkestan. The eastern group comprises the Turco-Tartars in the Tobolsk and Tomsk area and the Yakut along the Lena.

Mongols are usually divided into three sub-groups. The western Mongols call themselves Kalmuk or Eleuth and occupy southwest Siberia and Turkestan. The eastern Mongols or Mongols proper are called Khalkha and inhabit Mongolia, while the northern Khalkha live in Siberia. The third sub-group are the Buriats and inhabit the districts around Lake Baikal.

The Tungus are found throughout eastern Siberia from the Yenisei eastward to the Pacific Ocean, and from the Arctic southward to Manchuria. The various tribes are: (1) Chapogir, between the lower and Stony Tunguska; (2) Goldi, called Tuan-mao-tze by the Chinese, on the lower Amur; (3) Lamut, along the coast of the Sea of Okhotsk; (4) Manchus, in Manchuria proper; (5) Manyarg, along the middle Amur; (6) Orch, called Chih-mao-tze by the Chinese, between the lower Amur and the Pacific coast; (7) Orochon, on the Olekma River, (8) Oroke, on Sakhalin, and (9) Solon, south of the Amur. Among these tribes, only the Manchus are well known in history.

The Chinese inhabit southern Manchuria, inner Mongolia and eastern Turkestan or Sinkiang. As small independent tribes in northern Asia, the Ugrian Ostyak, along the Ob and the Yenisei Rivers, and the Vogul,

---

[1] A. H. Fisher, *The Russian Fur Trade*, 1550–1700, (Berkeley & Los Angeles: University of California Press, 1943), pp. 17–28.

between the middle Ob and the Urals, belong to the Finnic race of Europe. In the Arctic region from the mouth of the Khantaga River to the Ural Mountains, and thence, in Europe to Cheskaya Bay, there are the Samoyed with its related tribes Yourak and Ostyak.[1]

Despite the above classification, no definite racial borderlines can be drawn. In western Manchuria and eastern Mongolia, Manchus are intermingled with Mongols; in south Manchuria, Chinese with Manchus; in inner Mongolia, Chinese with Mongols, as well as the former two with the Manchus; in eastern Turkestan, Chinese with Turks, and Turko-Chinese with Mongols; and in western Turkestan and southwestern Siberia, Mongols with Turks. The Kalmuk, for example, are of Turko-Mongol blood. The population of the area is small because of the limited food supply, but it is denser in the south especially in agriculture zones. People in northern Siberia, which is almost barren, live by fishing and hunting; in southern Siberia, the Mongolian Plateau and the Turkestan Steppes, by cattle-breeding, with a little agriculture; in Manchuria and some parts of inner Mongolia and southern Turkestan, by settled agriculture. Nomads and settled agriculturists are better organized than the fishing and hunting peoples. Therefore, up to the seventeenth century, people of the southern part of northern Asia usually were the rulers of the whole of northern Asia; and Mongols, Chinese, Turks and Manchus ruled the area in turn or at times were co-rulers of the area.

In view of the geographical conditions described above, we may sum up the influence of geography on the historical development of northern Asia. With the impassable Arctic and Pacific Oceans on the north and east, the possible contacts of the area with the rest of the world must be through the west and south. The Urals on the west rise in gentle slopes and are intersected by valleys and easy passes. They therefore form no real obstacle to communication between Europe and Asia. Although in the south mountains and deserts form the boundary, they have not prevented people in northern Asia from reaching southern Asia. They have reached Persia and Afghanistan through the low lands of Turkestan, China through the passes of the lower Tien Shan ranges and the trails of the narrower Gobi Desert and the Khingan Mountains. Since the steppe zones are contiguous to these passable western and southern boundaries, they have lured the nomadic people to invade the Russian plain in the west and Persia and China proper in the south. On the other hand the forest zones used to

[1] Czaplicka, *op. cit.*, pp. 13–22.

be havens for those people who escaped from nomadic invaders. The other geographic factor to influence history is the net of waterways. The main rivers with their tributaries form an exceptionally convenient system of inland waterways. These were important communication and transportation channels, particularly during the early period of Russian colonizing in Siberia.[1] With this geographical background in mind, let us turn to deal with the historical developments of the area.

2. HISTORICAL BACKGROUND

In early times European Russia was invaded successively by tribes from Asia. Some Indo-Iranian tribes, the Simerians and Scythians (sixth century B.C.) and the Sarmatians (third century B.C.) appeared on the Russian plain. Later, when the decaying Roman Empire afforded temptations for loot, these tribes were followed by numerous others from Asia such as the Yazigi, the Roxaland, the Alani (all of Sarmatian stock), the Bastarni, the Dacians, and the Getae. Each forced the other to move westward. For centuries Russia was the victim of the invasion of tribes from Asia. Among the Asiatic tribes, the warlike and restless Turko-Mongol, with Finnic tribes of Europe as their western branch and Manchus as their eastern branch, formed the most dangerous reserve of man-power ready at any time to change the course of history by the pressure of their attacks.[2]

Since the second century B.C., when the Chinese emissary Chang Ch'ien reached Bukhara, China has been interested in the trade routes of Central Asia, and has fought much to control them. In the first century A.D., Pan Ch'ao, "the greatest of the soldier-statesmen who ever served China's Central Asian policy," extended his conquests beyond the Pamirs. His lieutenant, Hang Yin, reached the Syrian border of Byzantium in 97 A.D. and pushed as far as the Persian Gulf.

The result of these activities, it has been said, was to set the Turko-Mongol tribes in motion toward the west.[3] At first the Nomads, pressed by the Chinese, started moving westward, but they broke against the resistance of Persia, because Persia was then expanding in the opposite direction. Pressed by the double advance of Chinese and Persians, the Turko-Mongol tribes sought the line of least resistance, marched north

---

[1] Lobanov-Rostovsky, *op. cit.*, p. 2.
[2] *Ibid.*, pp. 3–4.
[3] *Ibid.*, pp. 5–6.

into the great wastes beyond the Caspian Sea, and invaded Russia. The great Hunnish (Turko-Mongol stock) invasion swept over Russia and under Attila pushed as far as France and northern Italy, while the Bulgars, a closely related tribe, settled on the lower Volga and the Don. Pressed in their turn by the Avars, they moved towards the Danube and in 679 A.D. under their Khan, Asparukh, crossed the river and settled in present Bulgaria.[1]

In the fifth century, a Hunnish Empire (Hsiung-nu) arose in the original home of the Turko-Mongols and knit loosely various tribes from Mongolia to the Caspian Sea. The Chinese had come to look upon these border regions as a kind of dependency. The Empire of the Hsiung-nu grew to be such a power that both China and the Eastern Roman Empire sent ambassadors to the Il Khan, and in 568 one of the Chinese Emperors married the Il Khan's daughter. The emergence of this power was naturally a serious menace to China, hence a constant effort, finally crowned with partial success, was made by China to subdue the Hsiung-nu. This caused more tribes to start moving westward.[2]

In the seventh century, a great change occurred in Turkestan. After the Arabs became a power and began to spread the Moslem faith by the sword, the Persian Empire crumbled and the Arabs conquered the lands of the Il Khan in the Central Asia up to the Tien Shan. The influence of the Arabs spread as far as the Ob River. It was these events which prevented the tribes of Turkestan and western Siberia from settling down and caused them to start their westward drive which spread over the great Russian plain.[3]

Thus after the Avars had established a great empire from the Don to the Adriatic Sea during the fifth, sixth and seventh centuries, the Khazars followed, driving them out. These settled down, losing their nomadic characters. They were followed in the ninth century by the savage and bloodthirsty Pechenegues and Black Bulgars, but in their turn they had to give place to the Polovtsy or Cumans in the eleventh century. Two centuries later, Jenghiz Khan established the Mongol Empire which spread over much of Asia. The Mongol armies conquered Russia, but this was the last of a long series of the nomadic invasions into Russia.[4] After the Mongols had conquered China and established the Yüan dynasty there, they played an intermediary role in making contacts between China and Russia.

[1] *Ibid.*, pp. 6–7.
[2] *Ibid.*, p. 7.
[3] *Ibid.*, p. 8.
[4] *Ibid.*

However, throughout the whole period of the Mongol domination, Russians remained adamant in their hostility to the invaders. Russian national unity was formed out of the struggle for deliverance from the invaders. The Slavs pretended to be submissive before the Mongols, yet they concentrated their power in order to overthrow the Mongol rulers. The Mongols had conquered the Russians when the latter were disunited. Later, in the same way, taking advantage of the dissension of the Mongols, the Russians liberated themselves from the Mongol rule. In the fifteenth century, Ivan III took the litte of Czar and succeeded in throwing off the Mongol yoke in 1480.[1] Thereafter, the Russians, reversing the westward expansion of the Asiatic nomads, were to sweep across Asia in their turn. Thus the eighteen centuries' rhythmical domination of Russia by Asiatic tribes came to an end.[2] The seventeenth century saw the Russians cross the Ural Mountains and subjugate Siberia. It was the first time that a European people had occupied the land of northern Asia. It is a new story that takes place in the seventeenth century, to which the following chapter will be devoted.

---

[1] *Ibid.*, p. 31.
[2] *Ibid.*, pp. 8–9.

CHAPTER III

EXPANSIONS OF RUSSIA AND CHINA
IN NORTHERN ASIA

I. RUSSIAN EXPANSION IN SIBERIA, 1552–1700 *

During the long centuries when Asiatic races dominated the Eurasian plain, little is heard of its present day masters, the Slavs. The first mention of the Slavs is as subjects of the kingdom of the Dacians on the middle Danube. This kingdom was destroyed by the Roman Emperor Trajan, and the Slavs then moved towards the Carpathian mountains.[1] In the seventh century, the Avars, then the rulers of the Russian plain, reduced the Slavs to slavery. Gradually the Slavs moved eastward into Russia and colonized the Dnieper and Don regions.[2] It is important to note that the Slavs came into Russia from the west and that their history has been a continuous movement across the great plain from west to east. In the ninth century, because the nomads threatened the trade route of the Dnieper from Scandinavia to Byzantium, the Norsemen helped the Russians set up the dynasty of Rurik which, through one branch or another ruled Slavic Russia down to the end of the sixteenth century. Under this dynasty the various territories occupied by the Russians were united into a powerful state of which Kiev, by the logic of its geographical position, became the capital.

But notwithstanding its brilliant beginning, Kiev was exposed to the persistent manace of Asiatic nomads. War with the nomads was a constant feature of the life of Kiev and sapped its energy. The ravages

---

* Cf. Chen Fu-huang, "Sino-Russian Diplomatic Relations since 1689," *Chinese Social and Political Science Review*, X (1926), 122–134.

[1] Lobanov-Rostovsky, *Russia in Asia*, p. 9.

[2] *Ibid.*, p. 10. Avars, a tribe of Huns, founded an empire soon after the middle of the sixth century, in parts of Europe then occupied by the Slavs who, for a time, were compelled to join forces with them in the war against the Byzantine Empire. The Avar Empire, of varying extent, had for the core the present Hungary and lasted until its destruction by Charlemagne in the beginning of the ninth century.

of nomadic incursions started a drift of Russian population away from the exposed steppe zone into the safety of the forest. Hence the Russian center shifted from Kiev to Moscow in the twelfth century, and Kiev crumbled in the thirteenth century when the Mongols overran much of present European Russia. After the Mongols declined, the Russians, with the aid of the Swedes, overthrew Mongol domination in 1480. The Czardom of Muscovy gradually developed with Moscow as its capital. With the fall of the Byzantine Empire, Russia took the position so long held by the Eastern Roman Empire as a balancing force between East and West. The marriage of Ivan III of Moscow with Zoe Palealogue, heiress to the throne of Constantinople, the subsequent adoption of the title of Czar (a contraction of the word Caezar) and of the double headed eagle of Byzantine as crest, were indications that Russia set herself the mission of perpetuating the imperial idea of Rome and the religious tradition of Constantine the Great.[1] When the balance of power between the Russians and Asiatic tribes turned definitely in favor of Russia, her advance into the northern Asia was to be remarkably rapid, and in a century it was to sweep across to the Pacific.

After the overthrow of the Mongolian regime, there remained three moribund Mongol states, the Khanates of Crimea, Kazan and Astrakhan. The first of these, becoming a vassal of the Turkish Empire, escaped Russian domination until the eighteenth century, but the other two were attacked by Czar Ivan IV (Ivan the Terrible) shortly after his accession. In 1552 he captured Kazan and Astrakhan fell in 1556. By these two victories, Russia reached the Ural mountains and the Caspian Sea and was in a position to expand into Siberia. The government soon made use of the Cossack communities which were springing up in the frontier regions. These were either peasants escaping taxes and military service, criminals escaping justice, or young men of rich families in search of excitement. Using the ideology of Russian nationalism and the orthodox faith, the Moscow Czars successfully enlisted these groups for frontier service. Finally they were organized into special "hosts" – both a military and administrative term. As Russia expanded eastward, new hosts were established along the shifting border. Though at times they were adventurous freebooters acting on their own and in open conflict with the central authorities, they rendered inestimable service to the Russian cause in Asia and were the leading figures in the conquest of Siberia.[2]

---

[1] *Ibid.*, p. 33.

[2] *Ibid.*, p. 37. George V. Lantzeff, *Siberia in the Seventeenth Century* (Berkeley & Los Angeles: University of California Press, 1943), pp. 54–63.

Once Russia was started on her expansion towards Asia, the motives driving her made the movement irresistible. These were first, the quest for security against the Tartars; Secondly the growing consciousness of a destiny bequeathed by the Byzantine political ideals, and finally, the adventurous quest of the Cossacks. To these must also be added the enterprise and vision of certain merchant families who carried on the great Novgorodian tradition of commercial exploration. The merchants desired to export Russian goods to the East and to import Siberian sables, Chinese and Indian silk, and other goods. Under the pressure of these forces the Russians crossed the Urals in 1582.[1]

In 1558 Gregory Stroganov, a scion of a rich and powerful merchant family of Novgorod, built his forts along the banks of the Kama River. Alarmed by Stroganov's expansion, Kuchum of Kirgis-Kazak sent his nephew Mametkul to attack the Russian settlements, and an open state of war developed along the border. The nephew of Gregory Stroganov, who inherited his domains, enlisted volunteers to build up his armed forces. Responding to the offer of the Stroganovs, a body of 640 Cossacks headed by two outlaws, Yermak and Ivan Koltzo, made their way to the Kama. Enlisting these men was a dangerous expediency for most of the Cossacks had black court records, and Koltzo had been sentenced to death for robbery. But the Stroganovs were in such a predicament that they enlisted them immediately, little suspecting that one of these robbers, Yermak, had in him the stuff of a great empire builder.[2]

In 1581, an expedition of 840 men under the command of Yermak set out against Kuchum. To protect his capital, Sibir, Kuchum mobilized a force about thirty times as great as Yermak's band. In the desperate engagement which followed Yermak captured Sibir. Under Russian occupation the name of the city, Sibir, was given to the country around it, which became known as Siberia. In 1582, a small detachment of Cossacks succeeded in overtaking Mametkul, the Kuchum's successor, scattering his forces and capturing him. This brought all resistance to an end. Most of the neighboring tribes submitted voluntarily and Yermak spent the winter of 1582 in organizing the newly acquired territories.[3] In 1587, Yermak's expedition built the city Tobolsk, ten miles from Sibir. After the defeat of Kuchum, the Russians came into contact with the vast new nomadic empire of the

---

[1] Lobanov-Rostovsky, *op. cit.*, p. 38.
[2] *Ibid.*, pp. 39–40.
[3] *Ibid.*, pp. 41–42.

Sungarian Kalmuks which centered along the Ili River including the Uliassutai and Tarbagatai regions and extending practically into Mongolia.[1] Therefore Yermak's war with the Kuchum was the key step in the expansion of Russia into Siberia.

During the last decades of the sixteenth century, Russia was plunged into a period of revolutions and anarchy, known as the Time of Troubles. Eastward expansion was thus suspended for a time, but before the armistice of Denlino in 1618 Moscow had succeeded in restoring its position in the East. A new Khan, a grandson of Kuchum, was appointed by Russia to Kasimov in 1614, and Russian expansion into Siberia continued. A number of new forts were erected, among others Kuznetsk and Yeniseisk in 1618.[2] By 1620 the Yenisei was reached and the city of Yeniseisk grew up as a fur trading center which attracted the natives for barter. Here, contact was first established with the Buriats, an independent warlike race, the northernmost section of Jenghiz Khan's Mongols. They barred further advance, hence the Russians turned northeast, and some ten years later the Lena was discovered and contact established with another people, the Yakuts. The fortified post (ostrog) of Yakutsk was founded in 1632 in an Arctic swamp with a dreadful climate. But abundant furs of high quality attracted swarms of adventurers. They later scattered over an enormous area of wilderness and became isolated and exposed to attacks of savage natives who subjected to torture those who fell into their hands.[3]

After the founding of Yakutsk it was discovered that the line of communication with the rear was exposed to constant attacks by the Buriats. Hence a Cossack *ataman*, Vassili Vlassiev, was sent with a force of 130 man in 1641 to conquer the Buriats. A long and ferocious war followed. On one occasion 500 Buriats were exterminated to a man. Finally the Buriats were defeated; Lake Baikal was reached; and Irkutsk founded in 1651. From these new centers, Yakutsk and Irkutsk, exploring parties radiated in all directions. In 1636 Buja with ten men pushed up the Lena and thence east to the Yana and Indighirka, discovering silver mines. In 1641 the land around the district of the present Nerchinsk was occupied, and in 1645 the Kolyma and the Arctic Ocean were reached. In 1647 an *ostrog* was established at Okhotsk by a party of 54 Cossacks who had routed one thousand Tungus and reached the Pacific Ocean. The following year a Cossack,

[1] *Ibid.*, p. 44.
[2] George Vernadsky, *Political and Diplomatic History of Russia* (Boston: Little Brown and Co., 1936), p. 192.
[3] Lobanov-Rostovsky, *op. cit.*, p. 45. Fisher, *op. cit.*, pp. 28–48.

Dejnev, with twenty-five men made a most remarkable voyage from the mouth of the Kolyma River on the Arctic Ocean, through the Bering Straits, eighty years before the official expedition of Bering. Losing two boats in a storm, he reached Anadyan, where he established the *ostrog* of Anadyrsk, the fartherest outpost from Moscow.

Further exploration proceeded southward towards the Amur. In 1652 Pashkof, *voevoda* of Yeniseisk, sent explorers to investigate the river Shilka with a view to establishing a stronghold on the upper stream of the Amur. With the approval of Moscow, he set out with 566 men and built the fortress of Nerchinsk at the mouth of the river Nertcha in 1656. The fort of Albazin on the Amur had been founded by Khabarof since 1651, but it was destroyed in the course of early Russo-Chinese hostilities. In 1665 Nikitor Chernigovsky, a fugitive from justice, fled to the Amur region with eighty-four other exiles, and rebuilt the fort of Albazin. The Csar readily pardoned their guilt and provided Albazin with barracks and officers.[1]

Okhotsk was burned by the natives in 1654, but was immediately rebuilt and thus the foothold on the shores of the Pacific was secured. Finally in 1697, a party headed by Atlasov, while making a journey on foot and with reindeer from Yakutsk to Anadyrsk, discovered Kamchatka. The Russian expansion in Siberia ended with the occupation of Kamchatka peninsula and a small portion of Alaska in 1700.[2]

The causes of the Russian eastward expansion have been explained earlier, but one more important factor must be noted. The Time of Troubles broke the power of the independent princes and the old aristocracy. After twenty years of civil war and foreign intervention, a new Russia emerged with the advent of the Romanov dynasty in 1613. The power of the princes and the aristocracy was taken over by a new social class of men of service, – sometimes self-made, sometimes descendants of the former aristocracy – which accepted the principle of service to the monarchy as the sole basis of its rights. This new and mixed class had decidedly capitalistic leanings and was interested in commercial expansion. However, until the middle of the seventeenth century, Russia was too absorbed in healing the economic wounds left by the Time of Troubles, and in wars to regain territories lost to Poland to show much interest in the East. The situation changed with the advent of Czar Alexis, the second Romanov. Now pacified and rela-

[1] E. G. Ravenstein, *Russians on the Amur*, (London: Trubner and Co., Paternoster Row, 1861), pp. 34–38.

[2] *Ibid.*, p. 46. Robert J. Kerner, *The Russian Adventure* (Berkeley & Los Angeles: University of California Press, 1943), p. 265.

tively prosperous, Russia was conscious of a growing strength and began thinking in terms of foreign markets and economic expansion.[1] That is, above all, why Russia methodically expanded into Siberia and sought contact with China.

2. MANCHU-CHINESE EXPANSION IN MONGOLIA, 1635–1697

For many centuries China, through its contacts with the nomadic people of Central Asia, Mongolia and Manchuria, had influenced developments in northern Asia. In the seventeenth century we find China in circumstances somewhat similar to Russia's. Early in the seventeenth century a Manchu tribe, being determined to inflict revenge on the Ming Dynasty of China for having killed some tribal chiefs, started to organize the Manchu tribes into "eight-banners." A strong tribal state was organized and it often raided the borderlands of the Ming.[2] At this time the Ming Dynasty was decaying after a period of power, prosperity, and culture. During the reign of the last emperor, a period of civil war continued for fourteen years (1630–1644). Taking advantage of this situation the Manchus invaded China proper in 1644 and proclaimed themselves as a new ruling dynasty. Although they soon pacified much of China it was not until after 1660 that all active opposition was destroyed.[3] Like the first Romanov, Michael, the first Manchu emperor, Shun-chih, was a mere child in the hands of an able regent who consolidated the position of the dynasty, but his successor, K'ang-hsi (1662–1723), like Czar Alexis, the second Romanov was one of the greatest rulers that China ever had.[4]

Before the Manchus came to power in China, they established a tribal state in Manchuria in 1616. The first emperor of the state was Nurhaci, later entitled T'ai-tsu. An able man, he consolidated the power of the Manchu tribe in Manchuria. His successor, Abahai, known as T'ai-tsung, continued the consolidation policy by uniting the Manchu tribes surrounding Manchuria and, in addition, started to expand toward Mongolia.[5] In 1635 he secured the submission of the Chahar Mongols and the next year compelled the Khalkha Mongols of Outer

---

[1] Ravenstein, *op. cit.*, p. 51.

[2] Chien Mu, *Kuo-shih ta-kang*, [*Outline of Chinese History*] (Shanghai: Commercial Press, 1937), II, 585–586. Chinese characters for all authors and books are given in the bibliography.

[3] Franz Michael, *The Origin of Manchu Rule in China* (Baltimore: The Johns Hopkins Press, 1942), p. 64.

[4] Lobanov-Rostovsky, *op. cit.*, pp. 51–52.

[5] Chien Mu, *op. cit.*, p. 586. Michael, *op. cit.*, pp. 60–63.

Mongolia to pay tribute. In 1637 when the Chasaktu Khan of Outer Mongolia raided southward towards Kuku-hoton (Kuei-hua), T'ai-tsung defeated the raiders.[1] Following this the three Khans – Gombo, the Tushetu Khan; Sholui, the Tsetsen Khan; and Subudi, the Chasak-tu Khan – proposed a "voluntary union" with the Manchu emperor and offered levies to support T'ai-tsung's invasion of Korea. In 1638, embassies from the three Khans to the Manchu court presented a camel, a horse, berkut feathers, and a Russian musket, the last item making the name of the Russians first known to the Manchus. From this time an imperial (Manchu) decree obliged the three Khans to present a perpetual annual tribute of a white camel and eight white horses, to be called the "nine whites." [2]

In 1647, Subudi, the Chasaktu Khan, and Ombo Erdeni, the Altin Khan, together sent a letter to the Manchu emperor expressing devotion, but it was written as though they were fully the equals of Shun-chih, the first emperor of the Ch'ing (Manchu) Dynasty of China. The Manchu ministry therefore rejected the letter and the proposals in it and issued a severe reprimand. In 1648 the Chasaktu Khan and Noman Khan went to Peking to offer submission and were entertained. Later the Altin Khan, Ombo Erdeni, who was a vassal of the Chasaktu Khan, made a raid into the Kuku-hoton territory and was defeated by China in 1650. The Khan thereupon submitted as a vassal of China.[3] Also in the year 1650, when they migrated westward toward Siberia, Lobdzane Noyon, Yeldeng Noyon, and another brother, Shukul Daitshing, chiefs of the Kalmuk Torguts, dispatched missions of homage to the Shun-chih Emperor in Peking.[4]

Therefore as early as 1650 the Manchu power of China was already established in the Amur region and in Western Khalkha right up to the Russian frontier in the Altai, though the Russians failed to recognize it. In 1655 the Chinese emperor appointed eight Khans in Khalkha (Outer Mongolia), namely (1) the Tushetu Khan, Chagun Dortsi; (2) the Tsetsen Khan, Baba; (3) the Nonum Khan or Dantsin Lama, the progenitor of the Sain Noin Khans; (4) the Merghen Noyon (Khan),

---

[1] *So-fang pei-ch'èng* [a collection of historical materials on the Northern Territories]. Compiled and edited by Ho Chiu-tao. No data of publication is given, but the work was finished and presented to the Hsien-feng Emperor in 1858. Chüan III, pp. 2–33.

[2] Baddeley, *op. cit.*, II, 112. *Shih-i-chao Tung hua lu* (or *Tung hua lu*) [Annals and Memoirs of the Eleven Emperors of the Ch'ing Dynasty], edited by Wang Hsien-chien, 1884, Bk. V, Ch'ung-te, Chüan III, p. 3ab. *So-fang pei-ch'eng*, Chüan III, p. 3b4a.

[3] *Ibid.*

[4] Chang Mu, *Meng-ku Yu-mu Chi* [Account of the Nomadizing of the Mongols] (Shanghai: The Commercial Press, 1937), p. 35.

apparently Abukha, the first Merghen Wang (Chief or Khan); (5) Bishirelti Khan or the Chasaktu Khan, Norbo; (6) Lobsan Noyon, son of the Altin Khan, Ombo Erdeni; (7) Tsetsen Noyon; (8) Khunderlentoni (?Khungdaidgi or Chief), Batir.[1] In 1656 the old Altin Khan sent one of his sons to the Shun-chih Emperor to present tribute.[2] Thus all inner and outer Mongolia became Chinese vassals.

During the reign of the K'ang-hsi Emperor, Mongolia was completely secured to China. In 1677 a conflict developed within the Kalmuks (Eleuths) of Dzungaria, when Ao-chi-erh-tu Khan was attacked by Galdan. Tushetu Khan of the Khalkhas gave aid to the former. However Galdan defeated Ao-chi-erh-tu Khan and then bullied the surrounding tribes. Tushetu Khan, Tsetsen Khan and Sanyenoi Khan, aware of Galdan's intention to invade Khalkha, sent a mission to report this to the Ch'ing court. In 1688 Galdan led a nomadic army of thirty thousand men to invade the Khalkha. The Khalkhas were intimidated by the fierce invasion of the Kalmuks and some of the Khalkhas proposed to flee northward to submit to Russia. In the council of the Khalkha princes, it was officially proposed that they should place themselves under the protection of Russia. Since the opinions of the princes were divided they called on the Khutuktu (Che-pu-tseng-tan-pa-hu-tu-k'e-tu), the highest ecclesiastical leader and real ruler of the Khalkhas, who declared himself opposed to the suggestion, asserting that the "Yellow Church" would not be protected in that case, and that they ought to appeal to China for their security. Thereupon, the Khalkhas agreed to seek the protection of China. After Tushetu Khan was defeated by Galdan, all four tribes of the Khalkhas went to the south to submit to the Ch'ing. In 1691 the K'ang-hsi Emperor went to the Khalkhas and told their thirty-five chiefs that they should not make war upon each other if they wished to have his protection. In 1693, six hundred nomads of Ch'e-ling-tse, a tribe of the Tushetu Khan, came back from Russia to submit to China, in view of the protection offered by China. In 1696 the K'ang-hsi Emperor led an expedition to attack Galdan and completely defeated him and his followers in Chao-Mo-to. In 1697 Galdan fled into the desert and died.

Having thus routed the Kalmuks and restored peace to Mongolia, the K'ang-hsi Emperor ordered all tribes of the Khalkhas to go back north to their original place. He also established a large army for defense

---

[1] Baddeley, *op. cit.*, II, 169.

[2] Michel N. Pavlovsky, *Chinese Russian Relations* (New York: Philosophical Library, 1949) p. 12.

purposes along the Ao-erh-k'um river which flows into the Selenga
River at Kiakhta. The army supported itself by cultivating land, and
the Emperor also enlisted many Mongolian soldiers to guard the Altai
frontier. Following the complete submission of the Khalkhas to China,
the Buriats of the Yenisei Region submitted themselves to China,
because hunting tribes like the Buriats, as a rule, were controlled by
nomadic tribes like the Khalkhas. As a result of the war between the
Kalmuks and the Khalkhas, China acquired dominance over the whole
of Outer Mongolia.[1] Later China continued its expansion up to the
Kazaks in Turkestan and came into conflict with the Russians there in
the eighteenth century. The role played by the Mongols in early Sino-
Russian relations will be discussed in the next chapter.

3. MANCHU-CHINESE EXPANSION IN THE AMUR AREA, 1616-1643

Even before the Manchus extended suzerainty over Mongolia, they
had established their control in the Amur area. The Amur region,
including the island of Sakhalin, had been under Chinese control since
the fifteenth century. With the decline of the Ming Dynasty, however,
Chinese control over this area became ineffective. At the beginning of
the seventeenth century the Manchus, who were to succeed the Ming
Dynasty as the ruling house in China, undertook the recovery of the
Ussuri and the Amur regions. The Manchus at first subdued the
Tunghai (eastern sea) group, consisting of the Warkha, the Khurkha,
and the Wochi, who inhabited modern eastern Kirin and Primarskaya.
In 1616 the Manchus crossed the Amur River. The Tungus tribes in the
area surrendered in large numbers, including the Solons, the Gilyak,
the Orondion, the Mangus, the Hegin, the Dahur, and the Kuye of
Sakhalin. After the conquest Yaksa or Albazin of the Russians was
built on the Amur.

The Manchus, however, accorded the vanquished peoples an opportunity of assimilation on the basis of equality with the victors. These
tribes were given status as Manchus and were designated as Iche
Manchus or New Manchus. In 1636 the Manchus reached the sea of
Okhotsk, which they named the North Sea. Further expeditions in
1639-40, 1641 and 1643-44 consolidated Manchus control in the Amur
area. West of the Amur their domination embraced the Shilka River

---

[1] *So-fang pei-ch'eng*, Chüan III, p. 41a, 25ab, 26ab. Pavlovsky, *op. cit.*, p. 15.

basin, including the city of Nipchu or Nerchinsk, as it is called by the Russians. It may be said, therefore, that by the middle of the seventeenth century China's northeastern frontier followed the mountain ranges of the Yablonoi and the Stanovoi to the sea of Okhotsk. If the Manchus did not advance further north, it was because their attention was focused on something far more significant: the creation of the Ch'ing Dynasty and its displacement of the Ming, south of the Great Wall.[1]

As a result of Russian expansion eastward and Manchu-Chinese expansion northward and westward, direct conflicts between China and Russia developed on the Amur in the seventeenth century, as we shall see later. It was the first time in the progress through Siberia, since the conquest of the West Siberian Tartar Khanate at the end of the sixteenth century, that Russia had come into contact with a large and well organized state. On the part of China, it was the period of the consolidation of the Manchus Dynasty's control over China. After the consolidation of the position of the Ch'ing (Manchu) Dynasty, China became stronger and stronger and continued to expand northward and westward. The impact of the two growing powers upon each other was inevitable.

---

[1] Agnes Fang-chih Chen, "Chinese Frontier Diplomacy: The Coming of the Russians and the Treaty of Nerchinsk," *The Yenching Journal of Social Studies*, IV, (February, 1949), 115–116; Arthur W. Hummel (ed.), *Eminent Chinese of the Ch'ing Period* (Washington, 1943–44), I, 2–3.

CHAPTER IV

THE ROLE OF THE MONGOLS IN
SINO-RUSSIAN RELATIONS

I. THE KALMUK SUNGARS

Between Russia and China lay the Mongolian tribes; thus the Mongols inevitably played a role as go-between in the establishment of Sino-Russian relations at the beginning of the seventeenth century. When Russia crossed the Urals and expanded into Siberia, she met little resistance until she reached the upper Ob, Irtish and Yenisei Rivers, where contact was established with the Kalmuks, Kirgiz and Buriats. These peoples, governed by a powerful aristocracy, and possessed of an effective military and social organization, were capable of forming effective alliances and organized resistance. At first the Russians were rebuffed by the Kalmuks. The Kalmuks or Eleuths comprised four main divisions: the Khoshotes, the Sungars, the Durbets, and the Torguts. At the beginning of the seventeenth century, the Sungars, who were about to achieve hegemony over the other Kalmuk tribes, extended their dominions from the Ili to the Irtish, thus becoming a dangerous and highly unwelcome neighbor to both China and Russia. In 1606, Baatur *Khungdaidgi* (chief) of the Sungars and father of the Galdan who was to be so famous, entered the Irtish country in 1606. He claimed suzerainty over the tribes in the neighborhood of the Tara, and the Russians from Tobolosk and other surrounding cities marched against him. Hostilities took place but Russia failed to drive them away.[1]

In 1608 on account of the war between the Sungars and the Altin Khan (a vassal of the Chasaktu Khan of Khalkhas), Baatur made peace with Russia and courted her friendship. In this situation the Russians in Siberia dispatched an embassy, under the guise of trade, to address

---

[1] Chen, "Chinese Frontier Diplomacy," *The Yenching Journal of Social Studies*, IV (February, 1949), 111-112.

the Altin Khan, and, with his help, to reach China, as will be fully related in the next chapter. Because of the Sungars' campaigns against the Altin Khan, the embassy failed to attain its original goals, but it obtained, through the Sungars, the earliest extant information concerning China as follows:

And to the Chinese Kingdom, it is three months' journey from the Altin Tsar, and the Chinese Kingdom has a stone-built town and courtyards in that town, like the Russians; in those courtyards there are stonebuilt halls; and he (evidently the Chinese Emperor) is stronger in people than the Altin Tsar, and richer. And in his court there are stone-built halls. And in that town there are temples, and in them a great ringing of bells. There are no crosses in the temples, and what religion they have is unknown, but they live like the Russians. They use fire-arms, and people come from many lands to trade with them, and they wear golden robes, and to him they bring all kinds of precious stones and other things out of many countries.[1]

In little more than half a century, the Sungars, utilizing the influence of yellow Lamaism and the violence of the nomadic tradition, became the dominating power in middle Asia from the Caspian Sea to the Great Wall and from the Himalayas to the Russian border. Tribes in the area such as the Kazaks, Kirgiz, the descendents of the Kuchum and some other Mongols were subjugated to the Sungars.[2] However, after Russia conquered the Ob-Yenisei region, she gradually obtained the upper hand in the rivalry with the Sungars. She could not tolerate the challenge of the Sungars for long.

In 1616, the Tobolsk *voevodas* Prince I. S. Kurakin sent Tomilko Petroff and others on a mission to the Sungars to secure their allegiance. The mission was also to obtain a guarantee that the Sungars would let pass any Russian officials going to the Altin Khan and China. Petroff's mission was to deal with the chiefs of the Sungars. When Petroff arrived in the Sungars land, he was told that the Sungars paid *yasak* (tribute) to the Altin Khan and to China, and that the Kalmuks (Sungars) owed allegiance both to China and the Altin Khan. Though the mission did not attain its original goals, it obtained information about the Altin Khan and China, allegedly from tribute collectors of the Altin Khan and China. The reports sent back to Moscow indicated that China was not far beyond the Sungars, that loaded horses and camels could make the journey in one month from the territory of the

---

[1] Baddeley, *op. cit.*, II, 34–35.

[2] *Ibid.*, II, 36. Baddeley uses the name "Kalmuks" in his treatment. Actually only one division of the Kalmuks, i.e., Sungars, was then the influential power in dealing with the Russians. For a clear description, it is preferable to adopt the name "Sungars" instead of "Kalmuks."

Sungars, and that from Tobolsk it would be three months journey.
They made no effort to reach the Altin Khan or China because they
had been instructed not to enter communication with China and the
Altin Khan until such time as they could obtain trustworthy information about them.[1]

2. THE ALTIN KHANS OF THE KHALKHAS,[2] 1616–1655

In view of the fact that the Altin Khans were influential enough to
claim sovereignty over the Kalmuks and because of their important
position on the upper Yenisei between China and Russia, Russia set
out to court them. In 1616, in spite of Tomilko Petroff's mission to the
Sungars, a Cossack expedition led by Vasili Tumenets and Ivan Petroff
was sent from Tobolsk by Kazansky Prikaz, ambassador in charge of
Siberian affairs, and Prince Ivan Semenovich Kurakin, *voevoda* of
Tobolsk, to seek out the Altin Khan. They were directed to take the
Altin Khan with all his nomad people and territories under the
Russian Csar's protection, to bring back substantial proof of such
submission, to make him pay (to Russia) *yasak* of whatever his country
produced, and to allow the Altin Khan to take the oath of submission
according to his own custom.[3]

Here we should refer to Russian policy toward the Altin Khan and
China which was found in a letter addressed to Prince Kurakin by
Csar Mikhail Theodorovich early in the seventeenth century. The
Csar wrote:

> We have agreed with our boyars not to have relations with the Altin Tsar
> and with China, but authentic information of all kinds should be sought out
> about them – how populous their countries are, what towns they have, and

---

[1] *Ibid.*, II, 38–39.

[2] The Altin Khan, meaning the Golden King, was a title given by the Kirgiz tribes to the
Khalkha Chief encamped on the Biduria Nor, near the upper Yenisei, to whom they were
tributary, because they believed him to be very rich. The founder of the power of the Altin
Khans was Tumendara Daitshing, brother of Buyandara, who was an ancestor of the Chasaktu Khans. The Altin Khan was a vassal of the Chasaktu Khan, but was more powerful than
his overlord. His influence had extended to the Yenisei region, where many tribes were
tributaries to him. The Kirgiz tribes, who for a time had declared allegiance to the Russians,
also came over to the Altin Khan as his dependants. The name of the Altin Khan who fostered
the first relations with Russia was Ombo Erdeni, or Erdeni Khung taidji. To the Chinese
the Altin Khans were never very important, and they were invested with the title not of
Khan but of Chassak. It was the Altin Khan Erintshin, styled Lobdzang Daïdgi, who
murdered the Chasaktu Khan in 1661 and thereby brought on the Galdan War. *Ch'ing shih
kao*, Chüan DXXVI, pp. 24b–5a. Henry H. Howorth, *History of the Mongols* (London:
Longmans, Green, and Co., 1876), I, pp. 455–457.

[3] Baddeley, *op. cit.*, II, 46–50.

how large; with what other cities they maintain intercourse and friendship; what their religion is, in what consideration they hold our great empire in comparison to other kingdoms and their own; are they at war with any oher State; what their arms; what goods they have; and with what other countries besides ours and that of the Kalmuks, they have established relations. And, if it be possible, send Cossacks or other people expressly to the Altin Tsar and to China, not as envoys and not as from yourselves, but making some pretence for their visit. Let them sojourn there, seeing these people's manner of life and country, their towns and their customs, and having informed themselves as to everything in accordance with our commands, let them report to us authentically. [1]

This policy was elaborately carried out by Prince Kurakin. As noted above he sent Tomilko Petroff's mission to the Sungars and forbade them to enter relations with the Altin Khan and China. In truth, however, the missions or embassies to Siberian tribes originated with the Siberian *voevodas*, who were really not effectively controlled by Moscow. When circumstances appeared convenient, they sidetracked Csarial orders, and so when Kurakin sent the Tumenets and Petroff mission to the Altin Khan, he ordered them to appear as ambassadors, to make their addresses, and to present their gifts, all in the name of their boyar, the Prince Ivan Semenovich Kurakin, and in the name of the Czar. But the mission was also sent by Ambassador Prikaz, who was in charge of Siberian affairs on behalf of Moscow, and the leaders of the mission, considering that they had been sent to the Altin Khan by the Czar, styled themselves envoys from His Majesty.[2] As a result, the expedition fulfilled its mission by securing the Altin Khan as a vassal of Russia.

When the Tumenets and Petroff mission were at the Altin Khan's encampment, they made inquiry about China. They were told that the Chinese capital lay at the head of a gulf, that the city, built of bricks, was so huge that it took ten days to ride around it on horseback, that it was a month's journey from the Altin Khan's country to China and people of China affirmed that it was very extensive, and they called their sovereign Taibin. They also were told that the Chinese used *pishehali* (muskets) and cannon, and that big ships came to China from over the sea with many kinds of valuable goods. Chinese goods were as follows: satins, velvets, silks. They also made goldwork and produced much grain. The country was flat, and the Chinese Csar was in communication with the rulers of all the kingdoms that neighbored his own, nor were there any wars between them. They had their own religion and religious service, but no one knew precisely their nature.[3]

[1] *Ibid.*, II, 51-52,
[2] *Ibid.*
[3] *Ibid.*, p. 57.

It is noteworthy that the Altin Khan forwarded the Russian mission led by Petlin and Mundoff in 1618 to China. The frontier was in a parlous state; the Manchus were attacking in force and the Ming Empire was tottered to its fall. For the safety of the mission, the Khan asked a Tibetan Lama to convoy the mission to China, because the Lama was acquainted with both the Mongols and the Chinese. It was the first Christian, secular mission to China, and it travelled there under the aegis of Tibetan Buddhism then established in Mongolia.[1]

The road to China from Russia, however, remained insecure because of the uprising of Siberian tribes, though the Sungars and Altin Khan had offered submission to Russia. Under such situations the Russian Csar lost no time in accepting an alliance with the Altin Khan directed against the Kalmuks, who had hindered establishing good relations between the two countries. The Altin Khan's proposal was made known in a letter presented by the Khan's envoys Laba Tarkhan and Ketibakshu to the Russian Czar, who went to Moscow with the Russian mission of Tumenets and Petroff in 1617. In 1620, the Csar sent a letter to the Khan, stating that the road from Moscow to the Altin Khan's encampment should be kept open for the convenience of their envoys and traders; that this desirable state of things, however, had been hindered by the Kalmuk brigands; and that consequently he had sent orders to the *voevodas* of Tomsk and Tobolsk, and all concerned, to send Russian troops with the Altin Khan's against the Kalmuks. The Russian troops should attack from the west and the Altin Khan's from the east, so that there should be no more of the brigands between Moscow and the Altin Khan's country.[2] At length the allies achieved their purpose.

In 1620, the year after Petlin returned from China, the Cossack headman, Andrei Sharighin, and the aforementioned *Ataman* Vasili Tumenets received orders from the Tobolsk *voevodas* to seek out a way by water, up the Yenisei, to China. As no reports of this expedition are traceable, it was presumed that the mission accomplished nothing. After that, there seems to have been no attempt for many years to reopen communications with China, or to maintain relations with the Altin Khan. Moscow reiterated its previous cautious policy of confining itself to obtaining information about various countries without entering into official relations with its Asiatic neighbors, because those countries were distant and it was too far for their merchants to

---

[1] *Ibid.*, p. 85.
[2] *Ibid.*, pp. 87–89.

come to Russia; moreover, the nomad hordes of the Altin Khan were warlike people and Russia received no benefits from them. Actually the cessation of intercourse with those countries, especially China, might well be accounted for by the state of things on the Siberian border, where the Russian settlers were harassed by Kalmuks, Buriats, Tunguses, and other tribesmen, but especially by the Kirgiz, with whom they waged incessant warfare.[1]

Owing partly to this state of things and partly to Moscow's cautious policy, the friendly relations established by Tumenets and others with the Altin Khan suffered temporary eclipse. During twelve years, indeed, there seems to have been no intercourse whatever. In 1632, however, came a change. The Altin Khan himself took steps towards closer relations with Russia, because he was seeking protection against his neighboring enemy Chaghir (Chahar) Khan and the potential threat from the Manchus.[2] In 1633 the Altin Khan sent envoys to Tomsk to offer the complete submission of himself and all his people. These envoys promised that their master would pay tribute, and, in case of necessity, would serve with all his forces in the field against the enemies of Russia. They begged an equal defense in turn against enemies, and requested that Russian ambassadors be sent to the Altin Khan so that he might personally declare his willingness to obey and take an oath of allegiance.[3]

The Altin Khan's new policy was in all probability dictated by greed and fear. The offer of submission was by no means honest. Moscow, however, was fain to make the most of it, and in 1634 sent Yakoff Tukhachevsky, with a secretary, Druzhina, to receive the Altin Khan's submission. When Yakoff and Druzhina reached the Altin Khan, however, he had changed his mind about complete submission and refused to take an oath in person, because the only reason for submission to Russia had ceased to exist – the Chaghir Khan, Duchin, had been killed by the Urtus (?Ordos) Khan and Chinese. However, the Altin Khan made a pretence of keeping his word. He expressed joy at becoming a Russian vassal, and ordered one of his nobles to swear, in the presence of the Russian mission, to make the Altin Khan's country tributary to Russia. The mission, in accordance with instructions, sought information about China. They were told that China could not be conquered; that it was a powerful country;

[1] Ibid., p. 73.
[2] Pavlovsky, op. cit., p. 9.
[3] Baddeley, op. cit., II, 95.

that the cities were all built of stone; that the people were numerous;
that beyond the Mongol land there was no other kingdom except China;
that the Mongols of the Altin Khan who went trading to China were
not allowed to go further than the frontier town of Kalgan, and that
they did not themselves visit the Csar Taibin, the Chinese emperor.[1]

Evidently Moscow set great store by the Altin Khan's friendship
at this time. Due to the growing power of the Altin Khan which had
brought many Kalmuks, Kirgiz and other tribes, under his protection,
Russia, in 1636, sent a mission led by Stepan Grechanin, again to
approach the Khan and to receive his oath of allegiance. Grechanin
read out to the Khan the Csarial instruction as to the Khan's submission and his duty to bring the unruly Kirgiz to order. The Altin
Khan promised to put himself under the protection of Russia; to
remain true and obedient to the Csar, and pay tribute, but he refused
to be a servant. He also promised to bring the Kirgiz into complete
subjection to the Csar. Meanwhile the mission learned that most Mongols had become vassals of the Manchus. The presentation of a Russian
musket to the Manchus by the Tushetu Khan made the name of Russia
first known to the Manchus.[2] The key to the attitude and behavior of
the Altin Khans towards Russia is to be sought in their relations with
the Kalmuks and the Manchus, whose growing power and very ex-
istence they had largely succeeded in concealing from the Russians.[3]

Russia, however, for the purpose of seeking a safe way to China,
continued its approach to the Altin Khan. In 1638, Moscow sent Vasili
Starkoff and Stepan Nevierroff to visit the Altin Khan and to ad-
minister the Khan's oath of fealty to Russia. The mission touched upon
the sending of embassies to China, the Csar's command being that the
Khan should first send his own people there to make inquiry. To this
the Khan answered: The country was already known to him in part;
his subjects travelled caravan-fashion to the Chinese frontier-towns of
Segra and Bayan, with cattle which they exchanged for silver, damask,
and cotton goods. The King of China was called Taibin; his place of
residence was very far removed from the frontier, and not every
foreigner would be allowed to travel there. He promised, however, to
get hold of someone who could answer exactly all questions on the
subject. In regard to commerce with China, an arrangement was made
– the first commercial accord under which the Mongols agreed to act as

---

[1] *Ibid.*, p. 104.
[2] *Ibid.*, pp. 108–112.
[3] *Ibid.*, p. 112.

intermediaries between the two empires. Henceforth the Mongol caravans which went to China to exchange cattle for silver, cotton goods, and silk, were to bring Chinese goods to Tomsk, which was to become the center of Mongol-Sino-Russians trade. After the audience, Starkoff, and his comrade Nevierroff, were invited to a dinner at the Altin Khan's *kudersum* (the Khan's palace). The drink was tea, and Starkoff in his *stateini spisok*, or official diary of his journey, stated: "They gave us an unknown beverage, which they call 'chai,' made of leaves from a tree or herb with which I am not familiar. They put these leaves into water and add milk to it." This appears to be the first Chinese tea known to the Russians. On its departure, the mission received the Khan's tribute, consisting of Chinese satin and silk, two hundred sables, and two hundred large packages of tea. Thus was tea introduced into Russia.[1]

In 1649 a Russian embassy passed through the western Mongolia and made contact with the Tsetsen Khan of the Khalkhas. Actually the Tsetsen Khan had been accidently discovered by Moskvitin in 1647, when he had been sent to find mines. He reached the Tsetsen Khan who told him that the Khalkhas had no silver ore, but that the Bogdi (Bogdoi or sacred in the language of Western Manchu tribes) Csar (i.e., the Manchu Emperor Shun-chih), who was very powerful, did have silver mines in the mountains, but that they were guarded against the Chinese and against the Mongols. However, the Bogdi Csar did allow people sent by the Tsetsen Khan "to mine for the silver ore" in exchange for sables. The mission of 1649 suffered heavy attack from the Buriats, but learned from the Tsetsen Khan many details about the Manchu emperor. It is highly probable that Baikoff's mission to China, which we will discuss later, originated, in part at least, from the information gained from the Tsetsen Khan.[2]

For several years the Altin Khan remained loyal to Moscow, and commercial relations continued normal. However, when China secured Outer Mongolia in 1655, Lobsan, the son of the old Altin Khan, attacked the Russian towns of Tomsk, Kransnoyarsk and Kuznetsk. When he heard of the death of the old Altin Khan, he hurried back to Mongolia, fearful of being forestalled in the succession. Lobsan did establish his authority as Khan and immediately reopened communications with the Russians who, in response, sent the former envoy Grechanin to undertake negotiation. Grechanin's mission was to secure

[1] *Ibid.*, pp. 113, 116–117. Pavlovsky, *op. cit.*, p. 11.
[2] Baddeley, *op. cit.*, II, 128–129.

Lobsan's allegiance to Russia, but gained little result. During his mission Grechanin paid a visit to the Khutukhuta, who told him that there were various foreign states on his borders: Bukhara, Yarkand, Kashgar, Turfan, Tangut, and China. He further stated that whenever the Csar might desire to send and make inquiry into the conditions of such countries, he would furnish the envoy not only with horses for the journey but with food and with guides. To this Grechanin answered that such friendly offers would be made known to the Czar.[1]

3. SINO-RUSSIAN RIVALRY OVER THE MONGOLS, 1665-1697

However, the Altin Khan's country rapidly came to a condition of ruin when attacked by the Chasaktu Khan from the east and the Sungars from the west. Lobsan was pressed up to the mouth of the Upsa, near Tomsk, where he addressed the Czar as father and petitioned him to build a fort there. After the submission to Russia of Lobsan the power of the Kalmuks land again shifted to the Kalmuk Sungars. Chokur and Senga were the Sungar chiefs with whom Russia had to deal. In 1665 and 1667, two Russian missions, led by Vasili Bubenney and Pavel Kulvinsky (respectively), reached the Sungars chiefs, Chokur and Senga, and attempted to bring them under the Czar's rule. The Sungars refused to submit to Russia, and both the missions failed in this respect.

Kulvinsky's mission related to trade which the Sungars agreed to carry on interruptedly. As to Russian trade with China, the Sungars agreed to furnish guides, food, and transport animals, in proportion to the number of Russian merchants, and to give them escorts back from Sungar's territories to Tomsk or Tobosk. Moreover, if any native peoples barred the route of Russian merchants to the east, the Sungars would suppress them, as the Altin Khan did for Russia before.[2] While at Senga's and Chokur's encampment, Kulvinsky sought information about China. He learned that it was a two months trip on horseback from the Sungar encampment and that no large rivers, bogs, or mountains barred the way.[3]

In 1667, Senga of the Kalmuk Sungars made a campaign against

---

[1] *Ibid.*, pp. 169-171.

[2] For example, As Perfilieff's mission returned from China, it was plundered in the Sungars *ulus* by Akhai-Danshin's people: The Sungar Khan assumed the duty of searching for the stolen people and of sending them back to the Csar, as we shall notice later.

[3] Baddeley, *op. cit.*, II, 177-189.

Lobsan of the Khalkhas on the Yenisei and beleaguered the town of Krasnoyark. Lobsan was taken prisoner into the Senga's *ulus*, but later he somehow fled. In 1671, Senga was murdered by his younger brothers, Chechan and Baatur, who thought to inherit his possessions. In this, however, they were disappointed, because they were overthrown and killed by the notables at the instigation of the Lamas. As a consequence, Senga's next brother, who had entered the priesthood and bore the name of Galdan Khutukhta, was chosen ruler of the Sungars (Senga's sons being minors) and received confirmation from the Dalai Lama. Galdan defeated his uncle Chokur and Chokur's son Bagamandschi in 1676. Bagamandschi's son, Chaidi, however, who was only thirteen years old, fled to Tibet, and in 1684 put himself under the protection of China. By this success Galdan became one of the most powerful of the Oerot (Eleuth) princes; he took in the title *khuntaidshi* or *khungdaidgi* the same year, and in 1679, when he had overcome and slain the Torgut prince Mafamamut and captured the Little Bukharan towns of Turfan and Hamil, he took the additional title Bushtu Khan.[1]

Such internecine strifes happened not only to the Sungars, but also to the Khalkhas. As early as 1669, Lobsan slew his legal overlord, Vanshuk Khan of the Chasaktu. The Dalai Lama immediately nominated Tsengun, the brother of Vanshuk, to the office of Chasaktu Khan. Tsengun collected his subjects as far as possible, but the greater portion of them had gone to the Tushetu Khan. Tsengun asked the Tushetu Khan to return his subjects, but the latter refused and Tsengun prepared for war. The Dalai Lama and the Chinese emperor made joint effort to settle the dispute and peace was temporarily maintained. However the peace did not last long and some years later, when Tsengun died and was succeeded by his son, Shara, the latter, in order to revenge himself on Lobsan and Tushetu Khan, made a close alliance with Galdan and actually became a protégé of Galdan.

While Galdan was concentrating his power over the Kalmuks, Lobsan, under the protection of Russia, attacked the court-encampment which Galdan had left behind. Lobsan not only secured great booty but killed Galdan's younger brother Akhai Dandshin. To avenge this and to restore the fugitive tribesmen of his protégé Shara, Galdan, after having brought Yarkand, Kashgar and other towns of Little Bukhara (Turkestan) into subjection, made war upon the Altin Khan (Lobsan) and the Tushetu Khan in 1680. This was known as the war between the Kalmuks (Eleuths) and the Khalkhas. In the war, Galdan

---

[1] *Ibid.*, pp. 190–191.

of the Sungars was allied with Shara of the Chasaktu, while the Altin Khan (Lobsan) was allied with the Tushetu Khan. The former allies were far stronger than the latter.[1]

Thenceforth Galdan made almost yearly campaigns, now against the Khalkhas and then against the Kirgiz. In this way, he drove the Khalkhas to such straits that some of their princes submitted to him, while others sought help from China. At this time Russia was preoccupied with the war against Turkey and hardly supported Lobsan. Lobsan, therefore, placed no great reliance on Russia's protection and sent a messenger to Peking in 1681 to render homage and to seek help. China had long recognized the Khalkhas as her dependents and promptly responded to the appeal of Lobsan. In 1682, a Chinese envoy was sent to Lobsan but on the way he received the news that Lobsan had been defeated and captured by the Chasaktu Khan and the Sungar monarch Galdan. The situation seemed dangerous to China; and she ultimately intervened in the war and backed the Tushetu Khan and the other Khalkhas Khans.

In view of the Chinese intervention, Galdan turned to Russia for aid. However, as a result of the conclusion of the Treaty of Nerchinsk in 1689, which will be discussed later, Russia was restrained from helping Galdan, and so turned down his request. In the meantime Lobsan escaped. In 1692, he came to Peking from Sining (the Capital of Tsinghai Province of China), and presented himself to the K'ang-hsi Emperor. As he had long been a *chassak* (chief) of the Khalkhas, the Emperor appointed him *fu-kuo-gun* (a title of investment). An arrangement was worked out whereby Lobsan came under the protection of China and was to dispatch forces to attack Galdan from the west while China would wage war in the east. In 1696, Lobsan took part in the campaign against Galdan and died while serving.[2]

At first Galdan experienced good fortune, even in his contest with the united forces of the Khalkhas and Chinese, but finally, when he had become formidable even to the Chinese, he was abandoned by the best of his warriors. These warriors, thanks partly to being tired out by the long war and partly from being turned against Galdan by the highest Lama, who found him not docile enough, went over to his nephew Tsagan-Araptan. Abandoned thus, and forced, in 1697, to flee before the Khalkhas and Chinese, he is said to have taken his own life on his

[1] *Ibid.*, pp. 191–193.
[2] *Ibid.*

way of retreat. The flight and death of Galdan was due primarily to Chinese intervention initiated by the K'ang-hsi Emperor in 1696.[1] Thus the whole of Mongolia was secured to China as we have noted elsewhere, and by diplomacy and force the Chinese triumphed over the Russians.

---

[1] *Ibid.*, pp. 190–191.

CHAPTER V

EARLY CONTACTS BETWEEN RUSSIA AND CHINA

Having viewed the background and perspective of happenings in northern Asia in the seventeenth century, we now come to consider direct contacts between Russia and China. Although some Russians were in China during the Mongol period, details of these contacts are obscure and need not concern us here. It is interesting to note in passing, however, that Grand Duke Yaroslav attended the coronation of Grand Khan Kuyuk at Karakoram in 1246 where he died, apparently of poison,[1] and that during the reign of the Yüan Emperor Wen-tsung (Tob Timur, 1329–1332) many Russians (O-lo-ssu) were brought to China as prisoners and were organized as an "ever-faithful Russian life-guard." This unit was assigned land for its support north of Peking and was to present game, fish, etc. for the emperor's table.[2]

I. THE ALLEGED RUSSIAN EMBASSY TO CHINA IN 1567

A number of works dealing with Sino-Russian relations report a Russian embassy to China in 1567 under the direction of Ivan Petroff and Burnash Alisheff.[3] Actually no such mission took place, although a report of this journey exists in the Russian archives. It bears the title "Description of Countries beyond Siberia" which is strange, since the Russian conquest of Siberia had not even begun in 1567.[4] The information contained in this report on Mongolia and China is contained

---

[1] Pavlovsky, *Chinese Russian Relations*, pp. 1–2, 165.
[2] *Yüan shih* [History of the Yüan Dynasty], Bk. VIII of the *Erh shih wu shih* [Histories of the Twenty-Five Dynasties], (Shanghai: Kaming Book Co., 1934), Chüan XXXVI, p. 93; Baddeley, *op. cit.*, I, 35.
[3] Ken-shen Weigh, *Russo-Chinese Diplomacy* (Shanghai: The Commercial Press, 1928), pp. 15–16 quoting Samuel W. Williams, *The Middle Kingdoms* (New York: Charles Scribner's and Sons, 1910), II, 441.
[4] Baddeley, *op. cit.*, II, 69.

almost verbatim in a report of a later journey, that of Petlin, in 1618–1620. The historian Karamzin, comparing the two reports in the beginning of the nineteenth century, concluded that Petlin himself never went to Mongolia nor to China and simply copied the report of the mission of 1567. It has been established, however, that the opposite is true. The information about Mongolia in both reports, especially the information concerning Lamaist monasteries, corresponds fairly accurately with the situation in Mongolia at the beginning of the seventeenth century, but not as of 1567. It would therefore appear that the date 1567 and false names were added to one copy of the Petlin report. Actually the names were not completely invented; Petroff accompanied Tiumenets to Mongolia (1616), and Burnash accompanied the Mongol envoys on their return from Moscow (1618).[1]

2. THE ABORTIVE RUSSIAN CARAVAN EMBASSY TO CHINA, 1608

In 1608, the *voevoda* in Siberia, Vasili Vasilievich Volinski, dispatched an embassy to address the Altin Khan, and with his help hoped it would reach Peking. The embassy was disguised as a trading company under the assumption that the danger of attacks and pillage would be minimized. However, it was prevented from going further than the Sungars by the war between the Sungars and the Altin Khan, and thus proved abortive. It is interesting to note that the trading company was organized as a government caravan, which practice was adopted in many later contacts between Russia and China.[2]

3. PETLIN AND MUNDOFF'S MISSION TO CHINA, 1618–1619

The first Russian Mission which actually reached China was led by Petlin and Mundoff. In 1617 Prince Kurakin, who had been appointed *voevoda* of Tobolsk the previous year and doubtless supplied with instructions and all available information regarding the vast area under his charge, wrote to the Tomsk *voevodas* announcing the dispatch of the boyar's son, Maxim Trupcheninoff, on a mission to China,

---

[1] Pavlovsky, *op. cit.*, p. 165: Baddeley, *op. cit.*, II, 69.
[2] *Ibid.*, pp. 34–35.

with one Cossack Ivashko Petlin as interpreter. The mission was to seek
information as to the kingdom of China and the great river Ob and
other kingdoms. Although it is impossible to attribute the origin of the
mission to Mericke's intervention after the Stolbovski Treaty, to which
we have referred in the introduction, it is difficult to believe that this
mission was wholly unconnected with Mericke's endeavours. In any
case it is not surprising that the result of the expedition should have
been eagerly looked forward to by the English representative in Moscow and forwarded to England with the least possible delay.[1]

In compliance with Kurakin's order Theodore Babarikin and Gavril
Khripunoff, Kurakin's subordinates in Tomsk, organized the mission
for dispatch to China. It consisted of seven men of the Tobolsk Cossacks with tent-dwelling Tartars and four men of the Tomsk Cossacks.
The Cossacks were given government wages for two years and supplies
at one year's rate. The mission was also supplied with treasure and
horses. Eventually Trupcheninoff stayed behind and Petlin led the
mission and achieved celebrity.[2]

The mission took place in 1618 under the leadership of Petlin with
his comrade Anamshka Mundoff. It started from Tomsk on May 9,
1618, and traveled through the lands of Prince Noglin of the Kirgiz,
those of the Altin Khan, the Chasaktu Khan, the Tsetsen Khan, and
ultimately reached an *ulus* of the yellow Mongols. That *ulus* was called
Mulgachin (probably Mongolchin), one of the *tumeds* of Kuku-hoton
(Kuei-hua), and in it was a princess Malchi-Katuna and her son
Archultatu who had charge of issuing passes for entry into China. The
mission reported that up to the Great Wall the land was Mongolian but
beyond the boundary line the land was Chinese and the cities too were
Chinese. Through the wall the mission crossed the frontiers into the
Chinese town of Shiro-Kalga (presumably Kalgan) which had five
gateways under one tower. In the tower sat an official from the Chinese
Emperor who examined the letters and seal of the princess Malchi-
Katuna. The mission continued its journey from the Great Wall
through Hsüan-hua to Peking where it arrived on September 22, 1618.[3]

In Peking the mission was lodged in the great embassy courtyard.
It had been in Peking four days when a Chinese secretary with some
two hundred men on donkeys came and gave them brandy and oversea
drinks of all kinds and said that "the Emperor has sent us to you and

[1] *Ibid.*, pp. 168–170.
[2] *Ibid.*, p. 70.
[3] *Ibid.* pp. 73–75.

commanded us to ask you what you have come to China for?" They told him that Grand Prince Mikhail Theoderovich, the Great Lord Csar, of all Russia, has sent them to make inquiry as to the kingdom of China and to see the the Chinese Emperor. He told them that without gifts they could not see the Emperor so they were not presented. It was long established Chinese custom that without gifts foreign envoy could not be received by the Emperor, and when the Russian envoys arrived in China the Chinese court made no exception for them. This was what the Chinese secretary said to the mission:

Our land of China holds the following customs – without gifts no one can make an appearance before our Tsar Taibun, if, now, with his first envoys, your white Tsar had but sent to our Lord Taibun some small thing; it is not important that our Tsar admit to his presence, but it is important that the white Tsar should send gifts to our Tsar; then our Tsar Taibun would have received you and sent back the equivalent and moreover would have made presents to all your envoys and dismissed you. However, the Lord Tsar Taibun will now give you a letter to your Tsar, but envoy our Lord Tsar Taibun will not send to your Muscovite Lord.[1]

An alleged letter of the Chinese Emperor was brought to Tobolsk and from Tobolsk was forwarded to Moscow by the mission. The letter, as preserved in Russian and translated by Baddeley, reads:[2]

Van-li [Wan-li] Chinese Tsar, two men arrived out of Russia and Van-li, Chinese Tsar said to those Russian people, come to trade, then go away and come again. In the whole world, thou, a great Lord and I, not a small one; let the road between us be clear up and down to go by and do you (Russians) bring the best you have and in return I will make you presents of good silk-stuff, and you will journey back, and if you come again, and with you people from the great Lord, bringing a letter from him, I will send him a letter in return. And when letters come from you, I will order that they will be received with the greatest honour and the people with them; but I cannot send an ambassador to you, Great Lord, for the way is long and they know not the language; but I now address my homage to you, Great Lord, and beg him to believe that, were it possible I would send my ambassador but by my custom, O Tsar, I neither leave my own kingdom nor allow my ambassadors or merchants to do so.

As an account of the mission cannot be found in the Chinese sources,[3] the authenticity of this letter is uncertain. However, there seems no good reason to doubt that the Russian mission reached Peking, and the letter might have been an imperial letter or a statement given to the

---

[1] *Ibid.*, p. 82.

[2] *Ibid.*, p. 72.

[3] *Ming Shih* [History of the Ming Dynasty], (Shanghai: Kaming Book Co., 1935), Chüan XXI, p. 37. *Ming Shih Lu* [Annals of the Ming Dynasty], the 46th and 47th years of Wan-li, Bks. 453–8. Liu Tse-jung and Wang Chih-hsiang (ed. and trans.), *Documents in Russian Preserved in the National Palace Museum of Peiping, Kanghsi-Chienlung Period* (Peiping, National Palace Museum, 1936), Intro., pp. 1–2, quoted in Chen, *op. cit.*, p. 129.

Russians by Chinese officials which was not written into Chinese history because it was considered to be a trifling matter.

There is another epistle supposedly written by "Djuhandi, son of Van-li" which runs:[1]

In the time of my father came merchants from the great Lord (Tsar) to trade; but now no merchants come to me. Now, when in my father's time, the Great Lord's people came, they saw the sun, but now in my time they do not come. If thy people should come to see me, they would be as bright as the moon in the sky, and if they come, I shall be very glad; and will be gracious to them. Thou hast brought me two elk horns, and I have given in return 700 pieces of silk and do thou bring me the best of things and I will reward you in greater degree and I have sent to the Great Lord and Zahi (?) thirty-two cups made out of stone. And the envoys of the Great Lord came to me, three men and I ordered those three men to be convoyed with honour out of my kingdom to the great river and sent to accompany them, 3000 men for one day's journey.

This letter is very puzzling. Djuhandi seems to stand for "ton-tchang-lon" of De Mailla, the eldest son and successor of the Wan-li Emperor, known afterwards under the dynastic title of Kuang-tsung. He came to the throne in 1620, and reigned only one month, so he could hardly complain of the absence of Russian traders. The letter was made public by Spathary in Tobolsk in 1675. Spathary said it was written twenty-six years earlier, which would have been 1649 when the Manchus were already on the throne. Moreover the name of Djuhandi does not sound like a Chinese name, and is more probably a Manchu name. Therefore we are inclined to think it was a letter from Manchu frontier authorities in 1649. The letter might conceivably have been brought back by Zabolotsky who was sent by the Csar to the Tsetsen Khan in 1649.[2]

Although Petlin and his people did not have an audience they succeeded in their mission of obtaining information. They returned to Moscow in 1620 and brought back to the Csar a map and an account of the country of China. In his account Petlin wrote, among other things, about China, as follows:[3]

The Chinese city (Peking) is on a level place having round it a river named Yuho, which falls into the Chermnoe [yellow] sea; and from the Chermnoe Sea to Great China [Peking] is seven days journey; and merchandise comes to China [Peking] in small vessels, in 'shni-aki', for large ships cannot come up to the great wall. Tsar Taibun distributes these goods to all his cities in China, and from the Chinese cities the merchandise goes over the border to Mongol land and to the Altin Tsar and to the Black Kalmuks and to many other hordes and kingdoms, and to the Iron King, Timurs Kingdom, Kesh or Kash, south of Samarkand, and to Shar-gorod [the Khutukhta's people] near Bukhara, and

---

[1] Baddeley, op. cit., pp. 72–73.
[2] Ibid., pp. 73–128.
[3] Ibid., p. 83.

from the frontier they ride with those goods out of the Ortul [Ordos or Tibet] kingdom of the Khutukhta and Lama and from the Chinese kingdom, from the yellow Mongols and from Malchikatu, Chinese and Manchus and the Khutukhta's people with all sorts of goods, – velvets and satins and damasks and silver and leopards and with irbizi [tiger skins] and Russian and black Zondenmi (?) to all kingdoms beyond the border, and those goods they barter, and buy horses, and those horses go to the Chinese kingdom and from the Chinese capital those horses go beyond the sea to the Mantsi as we say to the Memtsi [western Europeans] and silver with them is in Kritsi [ingots] each Kritz 54 roubles, and 5 and 3 and 2 roubles and a grivnik; or as we say, a rouble; as they say, a lian.

There are many merchants and soldiers in China and they use fire-arms; and they wage war with the yellow Mongols; and the Mongols use bows for fighting and in China the people are timid.

In addition to information about China, the mission made inquiry about the great river Ob, which both the English and Russians attempted to exploit as navigable a water route for trade with China. The mission asked the Chinese secretary about the Ob and he told them he knew nothing about such a river. They later asked the Buriat peasants, the Tartar, the Kushtan in Kalga, and these people said there was a river named Karatala which might possibly fall into the Ob.[1]

Since none of the events treated in this section can be found in the Chinese materials, we are not absolutely certain that such a mission reached Peking. Probably, however, the Russians reached Peking, although they were not given an audience. They may have come to Peking among the Mongols who came to pay tribute to China. The tributary Mongols were seldom given an imperial audience, but were usually handled by the officials in charge of "barbarian affairs." The Russians coming to Peking might have been treated in the same way, and probably were given letters by such officials. They brought these back to Moscow as official replies, but in China, since the ambassadors were not received by the emperor, the mission would have been considered insignificant and thus was not written into history. Chinese history officially records Russian missions, starting with the mission of Baikoff in 1655.

4. SINO-RUSSIAN CONFLICT ON THE AMUR, 1643–1676 [2]

Although the Petlin mission failed to establish permanent contact between Russia and China, Russian expansion into the Amur area, at

[1] *Ibid.*, pp. 83–89.
[2] Cf. Chen, *Chinese Social and Political Science Review*, X (1926), 134–142.

the moment when the Manchus were moving into China, established permanent contacts which brought friction and conflict. Soon after the Yakutsk district was organized in 1632, the Russians, in following up the sources of the Lena, heard reports of the grain and silver supplies to be found along the Amur River. To solve the food problem of Ya-kutsk, Peter Petrovich Galovin, *voevoda* of Yakutsk resolved to have the Amur River explored. In July, 1643, Poyarksf and his company were dispatched from Yakutsk to the Amur. Coming from the rivers Dzeya and Brianda, they arrived at the mouth of the Olekma and met the native Daurians, a tribute tribe of the Manchus. Though the natives attacked the Russians, the journey was continued without loss of time. They reached the rivers Sungari and Usuri and, in 1645, occupied Albazin which was later recovered by the Daurians and Chinese.

In 1649 the second expedition commanded by Yarka Pavlov Khabarof was sent by Diniṭu Franzebetof, the new *voevoda* of Yakutsk, to force the inhabitants of the Amur to pay tribute to Russia. Going by way of the Olekma (Umlekam), Khabarof had no great difficulty in reaching and in crossing the mountains. The inhabitants on the Amur deserted their villages, being deeply impressed with Khabarof's torture, abduction, death, and cannibalisms.[1] An attempt to overtake them proved futile, and the Russians found only deserted and burned Daurian settlements. Well satisfied with his preliminary journey, Kharbarof, with a few men, returned to Yakutsk where he arrived in March, 1650. Those remaining behind collected from the neighboring tribes tribute which, together with some samples of wheat grown on the Amur, were forwarded by way of Yakutsk to Moscow.[2]

Khabarof reported to the *voevoda* in Yakutsk that if the country of the Amur were conquered, Yakutsk could have all the grain it needed. The *voevoda* was pleased by Khabarof's report and reinforced his expedition. Khabarof hastened back to the Amur, with the intention of exploring that river to its mouth. In 1651 Khabarof's expedition moved down the Amur on a number of barges and encountered the resistance of the Daurians at various places along the river. The Dau-rian garrison at Fort Lavkais, the site of the later Albazin, had been reinforced by fifty Chinese horsemen whom the Shun-chih Emperor had sent to collect tribute. Trusting to their superior numbers, the Daurians

[1] F. A. Golder, *Russian Expansion on the Pacific*, 1641–1850 (Cleveland: Arthur H. Clark Co., 1914), p. 40.

[2] F. G. Ravenstein, *op. cit.*, pp. 9–16; Tsiang Ting-fu, "Tsui-chin san-pai-nien tung-pei wai-huan shih" [A History of Foreign Invasions into Manchuria in the Recent Three Hundred Years], Pt. 1, *Tsinghua Journal* VIII, (Peiping: December, 1932), 6–9.

attempted to prevent the landing of the Russians; but they were defeated and retired, as did the Chinese force. The Russians as conquerors, resolved to stay there for some time. After a time the Chinese Mandarin (probably the governor of Ninguta) returned in company with the soldiers who had fled at the beginning of the battle, and expressed a desire to live on friendly terms with the Russians. This understanding might have brought tranquility to the border, except that Russian greed for tribute from the natives caused continuous disputes. Khabarof sent messengers in different direction calling upon the natives to pay tribute. Few responded to the call and many fled. Khabarof used light boats to reach the spots where the natives took refuge. When the Russians arrived, the natives could neither fight nor run away, and were captured. They pleaded that they had just paid tribute to China and had very little left, but they agreed to give the little they had to regain their liberty and promised many other things which Khabarof had demanded. Khabarof proceeded down the river, passing, on the way, the mouth of the Sungari and the country of the pastoral Ducheri, killing many of them and taking their families and property with him. During the winter the Russians fortified a camp near the site of the present town of Khabarovsk where the Ducheri and other natives attacked them. The Russians drove away the natives and then enjoyed themselves.[2]

During these years the Manchus were busily engaged in establishing their control in China proper, and hence the Oronchon, the Dahur, the Hejin, the Giliak, and the other Amur tribes were left to suffer at the hands of the Russians. By 1652 the Manchus had regained sufficient internal stability to direct some attention to the Manchurian frontier. A Chinese force was sent there and encountered the Russian expedition, resulting in the first conflict between Russia and China.

The Russians, well provided with the necessities of life, believed themselves safe, and were ignorant of the fact that a Chinese army was moving against them. Khabarof's campaign of 1650 and 1651 had caused so much suffering among the Dauri and the Ducheri that they, in the early fall or late summer of 1651, sent their leading men to the Manchu officer in charge of the Amur, Governor Uchurva at Nadimni, to lay before him the true state of affairs and to petition that China either protect them or allow them to come under Russian jurisdiction. Their petition was forwarded to Peking, and orders were sent from there through Uchurva, that Izenei (Hai-se in Chinese) the governor of

---

[1] Tsiang, *op. cit.*, pp. 8–9. Ravenstein, *op. cit.*, pp. 15–19.

Ninguta, on the Sungari, should assemble an army, march against the Russians, and take them alive if possible. Izenei, full of confidence, gathered about him 2,020 horsemen armed with bows or matchlocks.

In March, 1652, the Chinese made their appearance before the Russian fort. At the beginning of the fight the Chinese had the best of it and for a time it looked as if they would carry the *ostrog*. It may have been that the Chinese commander was over-confident, or it may have been in obedience to the instructions that he ordered his soldiers not to kill or injur the Russians, but to take them alive. When the Russians became aware of this situation they determined not to be taken alive and charged the Chinese bravely and gradually drove them back. No army can retain the field while it is not allowed to fire upon its enemy. Thus, the Chinese soldiers became demoralized and retreated. Although they were forced to withdraw from the field, their fight was not without important consequences. It checked the boldness of the Russians and filled them with fear. From now on nearly every report to the Russian higher officers had a statement to the effect that, owing to a rumor that the Chinese were in the neighborhood, the Cossacks did not dare go here or there.

Khabarof was a great leader of the Cossacks, but he did no good for his country. He adventured for private benefit, so that he treated the natives cruelly and levied tribute on them to an unlimited extent. Eventually he lost control over his men due to the unfair distribution of spoils. It is deplorable that Russian policy was to leave such an enterprise in the hands of private adventurers.[1] In the Chinese records the whole affair is condensed into one sentence: "In the ninth year of Emperor Shun-chih [1652], Hai-se, the general at Ninguta dispatched troops to attack the Locha [2] at the village of Ujala, but suffered a minor defeat." [3] No details have been specified.

Exaggerated reports of the riches of the Amur and of the achievements there led Russia to plan to send an army of 3,000 men to occupy the newly explored territory, which was to be commanded by Prince Ivan Ivenovich Lobanof-Rostoskoi. Dimitri Ivanof Zinovief was sent in advance from Moscow with a small body of troops to prepare the way. In the late summer or early September, 1653, Zinovief came to

---

[1] Ravenstein, *op. cit.*, pp. 20–22.

[2] Locha which means rabble was the name given the Cossacks by the Manchu tribes on the Amur. At first the Chinese probably took the Locha as but another wandering tribe on the northern frontier.

[3] Ping-ting lo-cha fang-lüeh [A Plan for the Suppression of the Locha], in *So-fang pei-ch'eng*, preliminary Chüan V, p. 1a.

the Amur bringing with him reinforcements in men and supplies, and funds to pay all hands, numbering 320 at that time. On his return to Moscow he took Khabarof with him; and in his place he appointed Stepanof, a man in many respects inferior to Khabarof. At the time of the transfer of command the little army was at the mouth of the Dzeya, where food was scarce because the Chinese Government had ordered the Dauri to abandon their fields and remove to the valley of the Sungari. The season being already advanced Stepanof with his company sailed down the river into the country of the Ducheri, from whom he obtained grain and within whose boundaries he wintered, being not very far from the territory of the Giliaks.

In the spring of 1654 he retraced his course and at the mouth of the Sungari he was joined by fifty Cossacks, giving him a force of 350 men. Either because he was ignorant that Chinese soldiers were on the Sungari, or perhaps because he felt strong enough to fight them, Stepanof entered on a course which Khabarof had in mind, but did not think it wise to undertake. In May, 1654, he steered into the Sungari and sailed up that stream for three days without a stop. A nearby Chinese force, with no orders to spare life, hurried to meet him. A bitter fight took place in which the Russians were defeated and forced to retreat, claiming they did so because they had run out of ammunition. The defeat had a bad effect on the undisciplined men. They lost confidence in themselves and looked for Chinese from all directions; and they failed to carry out the orders to build several forts on the Dzeya for fear of the enemy. But to meet the needs of a winter camp they built a fort Khumarsk at the mouth of Khumar River. After their victory the Chinese slowly followed the Russians with the intention of driving them still further up the stream.[1]

In March, 1655, Lieutenant-general Ming-an-ta-li, with his forces, came to the Amur. He attacked and beseiged the Russians with some success at Khumarsk and other places until April, but being unable to take Khumarsk and being short of provisions, he retired after destroying the boats outside the fort.[2] In the meantime Zinovief had arrived at Moscow, and, though the proposed expedition under Rostovskoi as originally projected had been given up on account of the disturbances which had taken place in Siberia, Moscow showed its solicitude for the future of the Amur country by sending a letter to Stepanof (dated March 15, 1655) assuring him of the Csar's special

[1] Ravenstein, op. cit., pp. 26–29.
[2] So-fang pei-ch'eng, pre. Chüan V, pp. 1a–1b.

favor and encouraging him to new enterprises. He was also directed to treat the native inhabitants with leniency, not to levy excessive tribute, and to avoid unnecessary collision with the Chinese. These instructions, however well meant, did not prove of benefit in the state of affairs then existing on the river.[1]

Pushed on by hunger and encouraged by the Chinese withdrawal and by the addition of fifty men, Stepanof, in the latter part of the summer of 1655 again went down the Amur and up the Sungari, where he was successful in gathering enough grain to last him during the winter which he spent among the Giliaks. Having failed to drive out the Russians, the Chinese resolved to starve them out, and therefore commanded the Ducheri, living at the mouth of the Sungari, to burn their homes and to settle on the banks of another stream in the interior, out of reach of the Russians. This move brought hardships for Stepanof, and it became more and more difficult to provide for his little army. Yet bare of food as the Sungari region now became, it was still better to remain in this neighborhood where fish, if nothing better, could be had, than to go up the Amur where bands of Siberian outlaws, one of which numbered three hundred, were in control, plundering on both sides of the mountains north of the Amur without distinction as to faith, color, or rank. This helps to explain why during the years 1656–1657 Stepanof confined his operations to the lower part of the Amur.[2]

In 1657 the Chinese government established the offices of Amban Janggin or general commander, and deputy Lieutenant-General at Ninguta. This was the first occasion that a permanent frontier military post was considered necessity in order to cope with the Russian menace.[3] Sarguda, newly appointed general commander at Ninguta, defeated the Russians at Shang-chien-wu-he. In 1658 he made preparation for a further struggle, which took place on the Amur between the Sungari and the K'u-erh-han Rivers where he again defeated the Russians.[4] After these two defeats, the Russians disappeared, escaped, or took to the hills as outlaws. In this one campaign the whole Russian force was wiped out and the Amur was freed of Russians as far as Nerchinsk. The *ostrog* of Nerchinsk was built at the mouth of the Nercha rivulet by Pashkof in 1657 after the exploration of the Shilka. He was subse-

---

[1] Ravenstein, *op. cit.*, pp. 29–32. Golder, *op. cit.*, p. 53.

[2] Golder, *op. cit.*, p. 53.

[3] Sa Ying-nge, *chi-lin wai chi* [Unofficial Records of Kirin], *Chien-hsi tsin-she*, 1895 printing Vol. IV, troops, pp. 15a–16b, quoted in Chen, *Yenching Journal of Social Studies*, IV (Feb. 1949), p. 121.

[4] *So-fang pei-ch'eng*, pre. Chüan V, pp. 1a–1b.

quently appointed Commander of all Russian forces on the Amur. After Stepanof's destruction, Pashkof removed his headquarters to Irgenskoi, and left only a small garrison at Nerchinsk.[1]

The Russians did not at once recover from his blow. For a time they were compelled to limit their activities to the region of Nerchinsk where they had seventy-six men in three *ostrogs*: Irgen, Telange, and Nerchinsk. As a result of the battles of 1658 the Chinese controlled the lower Amur, and once seven of their junks came as far as Tongamski Gulf (Okhotsk Sea) to make inquiries as to the movements of the Russians, and it was rumored that seventy more of their boats were at the mouth of the Amur.[2]

In the same year, Russia dispatched Perfilieff and Ablin's mission to China to secure the guarantee that both countries would refrain themselves from attacking each other in the future and consequently to ask China to release Baikoff who had been sent to China by the Csar in 1653 and was now rumored to be detained on account of the Russian invasion on the Amur. In 1660, Bahai, son of Sarguda, scored an overwhelming victory over the Russians at Ku-fa-tan tsun. The Russians abandoned the Amur altogether. Finding the field clear, the Chinese must have concluded that their troubles from the Russians were at an end, and therefore the troops were withdrawn.[3] This was a sad mistake and indicated that China had not yet got the measure of the Russians, who left undisturbed, gradually returned and became stronger than ever before.

In 1663 Russian adventurers under Nikofov Chernigovsky, who with other Cossacks killed the *voevoda* of Ilimsk and fled southward, crossed the mountains, came down the Amur, and settled upon the site of Albazin village. Albazin was rebuilt and served as a frontier *ostrog* on the Amur below Nerchinsk. By the end of 1664 there were 124 Russians in the neighborhood of Nerchinsk; and during each succeeding year their number was greatly augmented by a noticeable addition from among Chernigovsky's adventurers. This was the cause of much of the trouble that followed. In Albazin other criminals enlisted under the banner of Chernigovsky, bringing their number to three hundred. Without consulting the *voevoda* at Nerchinsk, Chernigovsky sent his men to extort tribute from the Dauri and the Ducheri. They appealed to China for help.[4] In 1665, more than eighty Russians intruded into

[1] Golder, *op. cit.*, pp. 53–54.
[2] *Ibid.*, pp. 54–55.
[3] *So-fang pei-ch'eng*, pre. Chüan V, pp. 1a–1b.
[4] Golder, *op. cit.*, p. 55. Ravenstein, *op. cit.*, p. 38.

the country of the Solons (Dauri and Ducheri). They exacted sables
from the Solons and debauched many Solon women. The Chinese
General Bahai defeated them. In 1668, Ivan and many other Cossacks
voluntarily surrendered to China. During the time many frontier
subjects of China fled to Nerchinsk and surrendered to Russia. Among
the most notorious was Gantimur, one of the Tungus chiefs. The
Chinese demanded the extradition of these deserters many times.
Especially, China insisted on Gantimur's return for the fear that other
tribal chiefs might by following his suit shift their allegiance from
China to Russia. But the Russians refused to surrender him. As a
result tense relations were created between Russia and China.[1]

In the Autumn, 1669, the Russians invaded into the Amur area
again. The officials of the Chinese court proposed to repel the invasion,
because the Russians could hardly get back due to the frozen stream.
The K'ang-hsi Emperor, greatest of the Manchu rulers, who ascended
the throne in 1662, was opposed to the proposal, on account of the
remoteness of the affair and his unwillingness to disturb people too
much. He nonetheless was aware of the re-appearance of the Russians
on the Amur. In 1670, he sent a letter to the *voevoda* at Nerchinsk,
complaining of the encroachment of the Cossacks at Albazin and asked
Russia to stop this lawlessness, without, however, demanding that
Albazin itself be evacuated. And in 1671, he ordered Bahai not to
relax the defense on the Amur in view of the surrender of many Russians, but rather to strengthen it. The *voevoda* was quite helpless in this
matter, and all he did was to dispatch the Milovanoff mission, which
we will discuss later, to Peking. Milovanoff returned with the Chinese
request that the men of Albazin cease harming the natives. But neither
the Nerchinsk *voevoda* nor any other officer had any influence at
Albazin.[2]

Another cause leading up to the renewal of conflict between China
and Russia was the renewed attempt of Russia to expand and to
colonize. Many Tungusians (the Solons--Dauri and Ducheri) in the
neighborhood of Albazin again became tributaries to Russia, and the
tribute taken from the natives was regularly sent to Nerchinsk. Upon
this China reacted promptly. In 1674, she dispatched a navy force
from Kirin to the Amur frontier. Russia was then engaged in a war
with Poland and Turkey, and therefore feared that this would lead to

---

[1] Tsiang, *Tsinghua Journal*, VIII (Dec. 1932), Pt. 1, p. 14. *So-fang pei-ch'eng*, Chüan LXI,
pp. 12b–13a.
[2] Golder, *op. cit.*, pp. 55–56. Ravenstein, *op. cit.*, p. 39. *So-fang pei-ch'eng*, Chüan LXI,
p. 13b.

fresh hostilities with the Chinese. One of the many purposes of the Spathary mission of 1675, which will be treated later, was to prevent the conflict on the Amur. On his arrival at Tsitsihar, Spathary is said to have admitted to a Chinese functionary that the Russians had no legal claim whatever to the Dzeya. On his return journey in 1676, he sent word to the Russians at Albazin, both from Tsitsihar and Nerchinsk, to desist from navigating the lower Amur and the Dzeya, and not to collect tribute from the Tungusians dwelling along the latter. Despite Spathary's efforts Russia still did not stop its expansion.[1] This expansion made inevitable the war between Russia and China in 1685–86, which will be explored in detail in the chapter, "The Sino-Russian War on the Amur."

---

[1] Ravenstein, *op. cit.*, pp. 40–41; *So-fang pei-ch'eng*, Chüan LXI, p. 14a.

CHAPTER VI

RUSSIAN ATTEMPTS AT ESTABLISHING
DIPLOMATIC RELATIONS WITH CHINA I

I. BAIKOFF'S EMBASSY, 1653–1657

As a result of her cautious policy toward China, Russia for a time suspended attempts to establish official contact after the Petlin mission of 1618, because of the extremely troubled and unstable condition in China caused by the continuous raids of the Mongols' civil war and the Manchus' attacks. After the Manchus overthrew the Ming Dynasty in 1644 and consolidated their power, China again became a prosperous and orderly state. Russia then resumed her approach to China, and in 1654 sent the Baikoff embassy to Peking.

Theodor Isakovich Baikoff was the first ambassador to China sent from Moscow by the Csar's own command. In 1653 he was dispatched from Moscow to Tobolsk by the Treasury with matters relating to trade and commerce. He was accompanied by assessors of customs, and was ordered to make inquiry, while there, as to what goods were to be bought in China, what kinds of Russian merchandise should be sent there and in what quantities, how far it was to China and whether it was best to go by water or overland, what arms the Chinese had, what commercial connections China had, and whether Russia might expect to get much benefit from intercourse with China. For these purposes, Baikoff received fifty thousand (?) roubles to be spent in Moscow and in other towns, in the purchase of trading goods for the Siberian or Chinese market. If goods were sent to China they were to be bartered or sold for silks, or for silver, gold, pearls, and precious stones. Later it was decided to send Baikoff to Peking, and a Bukharan, Babur Elubobayeff, was sent from Moscow to Tobolsk with the necessary orders and with a letter from the Csar to the Manchu ruler.[1]

This letter, dated February 11, 1654, set forth the Csar's descent

[1] Baddeley, *op. cit.*, p. 132.

from Caesar Augustus and the Grand Prince Rurik, and mentioned the renown of his ancestors in all countries and the relations he maintained by correspondence with neighboring kingdoms. It explained that because no previous ambassadors had been exchanged, the Csar was unable to address the Bogdikhan (Chinese emperor) by the proper titles, but that in the future if the emperor would write to the Csar or send his own envoy, his titles would in the future be set forth fully and in the proper style. The Czar desire to become firm friends with the Emperor and to maintain intercourse with him; he wished also that the *dvorian* Baikoff would be dispatched again on his homeward journey without delay. The style of this letter may be illustrated by a quotation.[1]

... with your name and title as you style yourself according to your rank, and we, the Great Lord, desire to be firm friends in love and in counsel with you, O Bogdikhan Tsar, And as you give orders to dismiss our dvorianin, O Bogdihkan Tsar, to us, the Great Lord, not detaining him. Written in our Regel Court in the capital city of Moscow the year from the creation of the world 7162 (1654) February the 11th.

Baikoff was instructed, first, to go from Tobolsk to the Siberian towns, and from thence via the Kalmuk *uluses* and other nomads to China by the shortest and most convenient way he could find; and in order that the Murzas and Taishas (the titles of the Kalmuk chiefs) might give him free passage everywhere, he was to obtain from the *voevoda* of Tobolsk, Prince Vasili Khilkoff, letters of recommendation, asking that he be passed on from one inhabited place to another. Secondly, he was not to surrender the Csar's letter to Chinese *voevoda* nor even to the ministers; he was not to enter at length with them into the object of his mission but was to reserve everything for the Chinese sovereign himself. Thirdly, on entering the Bogdikhan's court, he was not to bow down either to the palace itself or to any threshold making the excuse that what they demand was impossible. In the same way, at the audience, he was not to kiss the Bogdikhan's foot, but if he were called upon to kiss his hand he need not refuse. Fourthly, having handed to the Bogdikhan His Majesty's letter he was to declare that he was sent to inform the Khan of His Majesty's state of health, that the Csar wished to maintain friendship and love with the Emperor in the same way as with other neighboring rulers; and that if any Chinese envoys were sent to honour the Csar they would be escorted to Moscow without having to pay any duty on their goods; moreover they would

[1] *Ibid.*, pp. 132–133.

be allowed free trade in Russia in all respects. Finally, he was to inquire
secretly as to the Khan's feeling towards the Russian court and as to
his intentions – whether or not he would send envoys and merchants,
with their friends to Russia. He should also find out whether the Chinese were pleased at Baikoff's arrival; what the ceremonial was for the
reception of ambassadors and what their customs (perhaps religion is
meant here); how strong the Chinese empire was in men and money,
troops and towns; whether they were at war with anyone and if so,
why; what valuable goods and precious stones they had, and whether
these were of indigenous production or imported and if the latter,
from whence; by what route could trade between China and Russia be
firmly established; how much duty was levied on imported goods;
what harvests there were of cereals, spices, and vegetables; and finally
what was the nearest road from the Russian frontier to China, what
rulers lived along the way from Siberia to China, and whose vassals
they were.[1]

Having received the letter and instructions on March 20, 1654,
Baikoff dispatched in haste another Bukharan, Setkoul Ablin, to
Peking, to announce his coming, and having completed his preparations,
set forth on his own more leisurely journey. The Baikoff mission,
consisting of Russian and Bukharan merchants went from Tobolsk,
through Tara and Tomsk and Kalmuk territory by way of the Irtish
River, to the Dobron Taisha, who was nomadizing on the Chinese
border. They reached Abiega and then passing, through Mongol
territory, they came to the first Chinese city of Kuku-hoton (Kuei-sui).
Baikoff sent forward from Abiega to Kuei-sui some agents to obtain
food and transport. But the Chinese officials at Kuei-sui refused everything, because they had no order from the Chinese Emperor; moreover
they stated that China had not asked Baikoff to come; nor was there
any object in his coming to Kuei-sui. They directed the mission to go to
Kapka (Kalgan), the frontier town. When the mission reached Kalgan
the Chinese officials also refused to supply food and transport, but they
sent a message to the Emperor about the coming of the mission.
Imperial orders were sent to Kalgan directing the mission to go to
Kanbalik (Peking).

Baikoff and his followers reached Peking on March 3, 1656, where
they were met outside the city by a delegation of ten or more, headed
by two officials. They ordered Baikoff to dismount and then bade him
fall on his knees and bow down opposite the temples at the gate of the

1 *Ibid.*, p. 134.

city. They said, "bow down, to our Tsar (Chinese emperor)"; Baikoff excused himself, saying, "it is not our custom to fall on our knees and bow, not having seen the Tsar (Chinese emperor); with our great sovereign the procedure is as follows: we bow to him standing, bareheaded." At that moment they brought tea, boiled with butter and cows milk, and said, "that tea is sent by the Tsar (Chinese emperor)." Baikoff did not drink the tea, but begged them to forgive him, saying "it is now, according to our Christian faith, a time of fasting." And they said to him, "if indeed you are sent from your Great Lord to our Tsar (Chinese emperor), at least accept it." Baikoff took the cup of tea, but having taken the cup, gave it back.[1] The kneeling and the drinking of the tea were merely the start of the troubles of the diplomatic relationship between the two countries.

On March 4, 1656 the Emperor sent his privy councilors to Baikoff with the command to take over, against inventory, the state gifts. Baikoff declined to turn over the gifts saying that it was not the Russian sovereign's custom, and that when neighboring kingdoms had relations and communications with the Russian Csar, they presented a letter of credence and after that friendly gifts. Those councilors said:

That is your master's way, not ours, and one Tsar does not dictate to another. Our Tsar (emperor) has sent us to you with definite orders to take from you against receipt, those gifts sent him by your Tsar. If however you are sent from your master to ours for purposes of trade (only) pray deal with those articles as you please.

And Baikoff answered them saying:

I am sent by my Great Sovereign to yours not for trade but as bearer of His Majesty's gracious letter, offering friendship and love and counsel; and also as bearer of His Majesty's gracious gifts.

To these things the councilors replied:

If indeed, you are sent from your great sovereign to our Tsar (emperor) with a gracious letter and friendly gifts, our Tsar commands us to take the gifts from you by force; but the letter he will receive from you, the ambassador, in person.

However Baikoff refused to surrender the gifts and in the end they were seized by the Chinese.[2]

On March 6, Chinese officials came and demanded the royal letter of credence; but Baikoff refused, asserting

I am accredited from the Great Lord to your Tsar and not to you, his officials.

[1] *Ibid.*, pp. 143–144.
[2] *Ibid.*, pp. 144–145.

The presentation of the letter was thus delayed for a long time. On August 12, the Chinese councilors came to Baikoff again and told him to come to the ministry and bring with him the Russian Csar's letter in order to be shown how to bow down to the Emperor. Baikoff refused, saying:

Not having been received by the Tsar, I cannot go to the ministry; moreover, my great Sovereign ordered me to honour your Tsar in the same way as himself.

And they said to him:

Then the Tsar (emperor) will give orders for you to be executed for not obeying his command.

And the ambassador then said:

Though the Tsar (emperor) should order me to be torn limb from limb, yet will I not go to the ministry till I have seen his eyes, nor give up the Tsar's gracious letter.

On August 12 or 31 (a more likely date) the minister of State sent back to Baikoff the Russian royal gifts, which the Chinese had taken possession of on arrival; and they also sent word to Baikoff saying:

Our Tsar (emperor) has ordered those friendly gifts to be given back to you because you have failed altogether to obey his commands; you have not come to the ministry, to the state officials, bringing the letter of credence; you have not bowed down in our fashion, falling on your knees .... and from whatever countries ambassadors come to our Tsar they, none of them, have sight of him; we, ourselves do not see him, but only the intimate people and the Uvans [probably wang] in Russian, Boyars.[1]

Eventually Baikoff was dismissed from Peking with the Csar's letter and the treasury goods on September 4, 1656. He was not furnished transport for the treasury goods, but was supplied with food. Baikoff said nothing at all and probably knew nothing of what was, perhaps, the main reason for his somewhat shabby treatment, namely, that even while he came to Peking on an embassy, the Russians were raiding up and down the Amur, as already noted. It must be remembered, moreover, that the Manchus had only obtained possession of Peking in 1644 and were not yet masters of southern China. Any failure to exact customary respect from foreign barbarians would have damaged the new rulers in the eyes not only of their Chinese subjects, but of the tributary peoples, some of whom were only just making up their minds as to what their attitude should be. For these two major reasons, Baikoff deserved the ill treatment he received, as far as the Chinese

1 *Ibid.*, pp. 145–146.

were concerned. Furthermore, because Baikoff failed to comply with Chinese custom, he and his mission members were locked up as in a prison and not allowed to leave the courtyard. They could not obtain information about China in any detail. Therefore the Baikoff mission can be described as a total failure.[1]

After leaving Peking, Baikoff regretted not having fulfilled his mission. When he stopped on September 13, at a place one day short of Kalgan, he sent a cook back to Peking to the ministry to again seek an audience. Baikoff told the cook to say that he had refused to submit the letter because he was obeying his Csar's orders, but that if indeed the Emperor never showed himself to ambassadors, then, in this matter, he must plead guilty for not having obeyed his commands. And now, if the Emperor would be so gracious as to order them back to Peking, together with the letter of credence and the treasury goods, he would obey the Emperor's commands in all respects. Having dispatched the cook to Peking, Baikoff went on to Kalgan, where he remained to wait for the news.[2]

On September 14, 1656, a courier reached him from Peking, and told him:

I am sent to you by order of the Tsar (emperor) by the state officials and they told me to tell you: From the road to Kanbalik (Peking) you sent your man to the ministry to the officers of state, they reported the same to the Tsar, who ordered them not to believe what your man said but to make enquiry of you yourself; will you in truth, go to the ministry, to the state officials, and take with you to them your sovereign's letter of credence, addressed to our Tsar? Moreover, will you fall on your knees after our fashion and bow down?

And Baikoff answered and said:

I will carry out your Tsar's orders in all respects; I will go to the state officials in the ministry and hand over to them the letter of credence, and bow down according to your practice; falling on my knees, with cap on, and I will obey all your Tsar's behests, as it may please him.

The courier wrote down these statements and rode back to Peking the same day, ordering Baikoff to remain in Kalgan till the Emperor's order should reach him. Seven days later, the courier arrived from Peking with the cook and said to Baikoff:

Our Tsar has not deigned to summon you back to himself to Kanbalik, for the reason that you moved from the place whence you sent your man to Kanbalik and went on to beyond the last town; wherefore the Tsar and the officials

[1] *Ibid.*, p. 146.
[2] *Ibid.*, p. 151.

decided: he who behaves in such a manner cannot be in his right mind; he professes to have been sent from the Great Lord, from the orthodox Tsar, but has not the slightest inkling how to show respect to a sovereign.

Baikoff returned from China by a different road than that taken on his outward journey. It passed between the territories of Mongolia and Bukhara (Sinkiang) and through the Bukharan cities of Kamil (Hami) and Turfan and went out to the Russian frontier towns in Siberia.[1]

The above account was, in the main, derived from the report of Baikoff to the Csar. A somewhat different version of what happened is given in Nieuhoff's account of the Dutch embassy which was in Peking at the same time. According to Nieuhoff, an ambassador from the Grand Duke of the Muscovities arrived by land, having been six months on the way, though he might have done this journey in four months had he travelled in summer instead of in winter. He had already been there the previous year (here Nieuhoff confuses Ablin and Baikhoff) and had taken back with him precious gifts in return for the sables and other furs he had brought. Permission had been given to the Muscovites to come again on condition that they offer their merchandise to the Emperor before displaying it to other buyers. The ambassador returned on this understanding and at first was received with much favor, he and all his people being allowed to go about freely, buying and selling what they would. A month later the Russians, having in the meantime conducted themselves badly – forcing their way into the brothels so common in Peking and provoking noise and scandals – had their liberty restricted, though they were still permitted to walk the streets from time to time. When, however, the ambassador declared that he would only give up his letters of credence to the Emperor; when he refused to "kowtow" (to kneel, bow and prostrate before a person in ceremony) to the Emperor's seal, as the law of China demanded, he was dismissed on September 14, 1656 without audience. He was detained outside the city wall for want of a passport from the Emperor, so that he was obliged to send some of his people back to Peking humbly confessing his faults and begging to be allowed to return himself and made amends, since otherwise he dared not show his face again before the Csar. The Emperor received his excuses graciously and next day the chief ministers went to visit the ambassador in his lodgings and to inquire into the affairs of Moscow. They asked, amongst other things, if Russia were a great and famous country, strong in ships, and also if the Russians were good soldiers and sailors and men of

[1] *Ibid.*, pp. 151–152.

good faith.[1] In light of this account, to the two major reasons mentioned above for the failure of the mission should be added the rigorous custom of China and the faults of the mission itself.

According to their records, the Chinese regarded Setkoul Ablin and Theodore Isakovitch Baikoff as two separate missions, for they mistook Ablin for an independent emissary. Actually Ablin was but an advance agent, sent by Baikoff to Peking to announce the coming of the Russian mission. Chinese history records the Ablin's mission as follows: In the twelfth year of Shun-chih, i.e. 1655, the Russian Csar sent a mission to Peking to enquire into the state of health of the Emperor and to pay tribute to China. Because he did not bring a letter from the Csar he was dismissed. But in view of the sincere desire of the Russian Csar to be civilized and because it was the first tribute embassy from Russia ever to reach China, the Emperor felt glad and ordered the envoy to be entertained. Moreover, the Emperor, to please the remote barbarians, bestowed gracious gifts upon the envoy and ordered him to take the gifts back to the Csar without delay. The Emperor also decreed that the Csar should dispatch a tribute embassy to China every year in order to reward the imperial grants and to show his loyalty to China forever. In the following year, Baikoff arrived in Peking. Though provided with a letter from the Csar, he insisted on presenting the letter standing, in compliance with Russian custom. Thus the Board of Ceremonies of China ruled that, since he was ignorant of the Chinese court etiquette, no audience should be granted him. The tribute was refused and the mission was dismissed.[2]

So far as these records are concerned the failure of the mission may be attributed chiefly to the discrepancy between Chinese and Russian court etiquettes.

2. MISSION OF PERFILIEFF AND ABLIN, 1658-1662

As an immediate sequel to Baikoff's mission, there was the mission of Perfilieff and Ablin. Ablin, the Bukharan, who was sent by Baikoff

---

[1] *Ibid.*, p. 153-154, quoting *L'Ambassade de la Campagnie Orientale de Province Unies*, etc., (A Leyde, 1665).

[2] *Ta-ch'ing Li-Chao shih-lu* (or Ch'ing shih lu), [Annals of the Emperors of the Ch'ing Dynasty], "n.d." Chüan CXXXV, p. 2ab. *Tung hua lu*, Chüan XXXIV, p. 14a. *Chin-tin huang-chao wen-hsien tung-kao*, [Royal Collection of Documents of the Ch'ing Emperors' Courts], in So-fang pei-ch'eng, preli. Chüan XI, pp. 4b5a. *Chin-tin huang-chao tung-tien*, [Royal General Account of the Ch'ing Dynasty], in So-fang pei-ch'eng, preli. Chüan X, p. 4b. Tsiang, *Tsinghua Journal*, VIII, No. 1, (December, 1932), 18.

to Peking to announce his coming, returned from Peking by another route and hence missed Baikoff altogether. He wintered at Ablai's *ulus* near the Irtish River, and, learning there of the failure of Baikoff's mission, he reported the same to the Csar and asked to be sent again to China to meet Baikoff and bring back the government treasure. The Csar accepted his proposal, and ordered a letter to be prepared for him to take to the Emperor. The Csar's letter, after mentioning the rumor that had reached him that Baikoff had been detained in consequence of Russian troops having entered Dahuria on the Amur to chastise the insolence of the local inhabitants, not knowing that they were Chinese subjects, proceeded to assure the Chinese sovereign that, in the future, the Csar would not send any soldiers of his to Dahuria, but on the contrary would instruct his subjects to dwell in peace and in friendship with their neighbors. The Csar begged the Emperor to do likewise and to send orders to the Dahurs to avoid all quarrels; he asked further that Baikoff be sent back without delay; and finally, requested that Chinese traders be allowed to visit Russia with their merchandise.[1]

Ablin, having received this letter, was on the point of setting forth when he was stopped by the arrival of the news that Baikoff had returned to Tobolsk. The royal letter and instructions were taken from him, and in February of 1658 orders were given to send to China as *gontsi* (an express messenger) from Siberia, the Boyar son of Tara, Ivan Perfilieff, and Ablin. They were furnishing them with a new royal letter to the Emperor, with gifts, and with money for commercial purposes.[2]

In this letter, dated March 16, 1658, the Csar, after vaunting the greatness and glory of his ancestors and stating that many neighboring sovereigns sought help from Russia, said that hitherto he had had no communications with the Chinese rulers owing to the distance, but, that having heard of the Emperor's friendliness to his neighbors, and the constant relation kept up with them by means of missions, he wished in like manner to establish friendly relations and intercourse with him. For this purpose he was sending two *gontsi*, to present his friendly gifts, to give assurance as to his own health and to inquire after that of the Emperor, to ask him to become his friend and to believe that he, the Csar, would send him any articles that might seem to him desirable; further he begged that in order to cement their friend-

[1] Baddeley, *op. cit.*, p. 167.
[2] *Ibid.*

ship, the Emperor would send his envoys to Russia; finally the Csar requested the Emperor to permit his merchants to visit Russia bringing all kinds of goods, in which case it was promised that free export would be allowed of whatever Russian wares the Chinese might choose in exchange.[1]

The two *gontsi* were instructed to buy as gifts for the Emperor forty sables, thirteen black and brown foxes, four lengths of good cloth, ermine "shubas," and some mirrors to the total value of two hundred roubles. For the Ablai Taisha of the Kalmuks they were to buy furs for fifty roubles and two and a half poods of raw tobacco. For other purchases a sum of five hundred roubles was supplied by the treasury, with instructions as to what should be bought with the money in China and for what Chinese goods the Russian goods might be bartered.[2]

According to the Chinese records, the Perfilieff and Ablin's mission arrived in Peking in the fifth month of the seventeenth year of the Shun-chih Emperor, i.e. June, 1660, with the Csar's letter. The presumptuousness and lack of courtesy of its wording, as well as the dating of the year as 1165 (?7168) according to the Russian calender, displeased the Chinese court. The officials concurrently reported to the Emperor that the Csar did not follow the Chinese calender and that his embassy should be expelled. The Emperor, however, decreed that although the Csar was presumptious and his letter did not suit the Chinese official style, yet as the head of the foreign country desiring Chinese civilization, he should be pardoned so as to please and ingratiate him. Even though Russia was situated far beyond the border and had not yet been influenced by Chinese civilization, the Csar had in effect dispatched an envoy to present his loyal letter to China. All this indicated his sincerity and admiration for China. The Emperor, therefore, ordered the Board of Ceremonies to entertain the envoys with dinner, to accept the tribute gifts, and to provide gifts for the Csar and the envoys. He also stated, that it was unnecessary to dispatch an envoy to Russia to present an imperial letter to the Csar, but that the Board should send a haughty letter stating the reasons why Perfilieff and Ablin were not given an audience. In compliance with this decree, the mission was dismissed.[3]

In the Russian sources there still exists the answer sent to the Csar

[1] *Ibid.*, pp. 167–168.
[2] *Ibid.*, p. 168.
[3] *Chin-tin huang-chao wen-hsien tung-kao,* in *So-fang pei-ch'eng,* preli. Chüan XI, p. 5b. *Tung hua lu,* Chüan XXXIV, p. 14ab. *Ch'ing shih lu,* Chüan CXXXV, pp. 2b–3a. *Chin-tin huang-chao tung-tien,* in *So-fang pei-ch'eng,* Chüan X, p. 5a.

by the Chinese Emperor informing him among other things that "the tribute thou didst send we have accepted, and in return we send thee our gifts and favours." [1] The imperial gifts to the Csar included twenty-five pieces of damask, three beaver skins, three leopard skins, three pieces of velvet, three seal-skins, and ten poods of tea. Of these gifts, the *gontsi* sold in Peking some of the damask and all of the tea, and with the money received, bought 352 jacinths, lals, etc. [2]

On the return journey they were plundered by the Kontaisha's (Akhai-Danshin's) people in Ablai's *uluses* in March, 1661, but at last, on November 1, 1662, they reached Moscow and delivered all that remained of their goods to the government treasury. [3]

From the available information it is evident that this mission, either profiting from Baikhoff's experience or because they were only express messengers, respected Chinese custom and carried out the orders of the Emperor. As a result they were entertained as tribute bearers from the Csar, their gifts were accepted and gifts were sent in return. The Chinese, however, mistook the express messengers as full fledged envoys, and treated them much better than they did the official envoy Baikoff. It was at this time, as already noted, that the Russians were forced out of the Amur, and for a number of years they made no more attempts to establish commercial and diplomatic relations, until the approach of the Chinese to the *voevoda* of Nerchinsk provided an excuse for sending a new mission.

---

[1] Baddeley, *op. cit.*, p. 168.
[2] *Ibid.*
[3] *Ibid.*

CHAPTER VII

RUSSIAN ATTEMPTS AT ESTABLISHING
DIPLOMATIC RELATIONS WITH CHINA II

I. MILOVANOFF'S MISSION, 1670

As noted above, one of the causes for the failure of the Baikoff's mission was the conflict between Russians and Chinese on the Amur. After Russians began again to move into the Amur, new difficulties arose which led the Chinese frontier authorities to open communications with local Siberian authorities. In 1670 the Defense Commissioner of Ninguta sent dispatches to Nerchinsk, protesting against Russian encroachments on the Amur, and demanding the extradition of Ganti-mur, a Solon prince, who, with his tribe, had gone over to Russia. In reply Danilo Arshinsky, *voevoda* of Nerchinsk, who apparently had little comprehension of the real situation, sent a Cossack, Ignashka Milovanoff, to Peking with proposals that Emperor K'ang-hsi accept Russian suzerainty. Although the Chinese officials, or perhaps the Jesuit interpretors, must have suppressed the offensive passage, yet such a demand caused China to impose subsequent humiliation on Russia.[1] Chinese records reveal the event as follows:[2] In the fourth month of the ninth year (of K'ang-hsi) Russia sent an envoy to present his *piao* (official letter) as a sign of submission, but the text of it was uncomprehensible; the script went from the bottom to the top, like the Taoist charm seals. Therefore, the Russian envoy was summoned to translate the document in order to present to the Emperor.

Arshinsky dared to advance such a demand, because he considered K'ang-hsi a petty prince who should be brought under Russian protection in compliance with the Csar's ukase to Alhanassi Pashkoff,

---

[1] Baddeley, *op. cit.*, pp. 195–197. Chen, *Yenching Journal of Social Studies*, IV (Feb., 1949), 131–132.

[2] Chang Yü-shu, "Wai-kuo chi," in Chang Ch'ao, *Chao-tai ts'ung-shu* (Collectanea of the Glorious Dynasty), quoted in Joseph Sebes, S. J., *The Jesuits and the Sino-Russian Treaty of Nerchinsk (1689)* (Rome: Institutum Historicum S. I., 1961), p. 65.

Arshinsky's predecessor, that the petty princes of the various Siberian tribes should be taken into the Csar's dominion. In April, 1670, Arshinsky sent Milovanoff, an illiterate Cossack, with Antoshka Fitieff, Grishko Kobiakoff, and three Dahur Cossacks from Nerchinsk to the Chinese Emperor along with some of the Emperor's Dahur people, who had come to Nerchinsk to trade. Arshinsky gave them written instructions, in reply to questions, as to what they should say to the Chinese Emperor: [1]

There are Tsars and Kings who own allegiance to the Great Lord Tsar and Grand Prince, Alexei Mikhailovich, Autocrat of All Russias, Great, Little, and White, and the Great Lord graciously deigns to extend to them his royal gifts and favor.

The Bogdoi Tsar (Chinese Emperor) would do well to seek likewise the favor and presents of the Grand Prince, Alexei Mikhailovich, autocrat of all the Russias, Great, Little, and White, and place himself under His Tsarial Majesty's protection.

And the Grand Prince, Alexei Mikhailovich, autocrat of all Russias, Great, Little, and White, and lord and possessor of many kingdoms, will in that case send the Bogdikhan gifts and keep him in his gracious royal care, and protect him from his enemies.

At the same time the Bogdikhan would come under the Tsarial Majesty's, the Great, Lord's, high hand for ever without fail, and present to him, the Great Lord, tribute and allow the Great Lord's people and his own, on either side, to trade freely.

And what the Bogdikhan decides let him forward to His Tsarial Majesty, the Great Lord, by those same envoys.

As to the question of Gantimur, the message went on to say, that since he was aged and ill, the authorities of Nerchinsk could not return him to the Chinese without the Csar's permission. Finally Arshinsky stated that the Csar had issued orders to restrain the lawlessness of the Cossacks, and instructed the officers at Nerchinsk to place them under effective control.[2] The mission proceeded to Tsitsihar on the Naun River where it was met by two Chinese officials and a Jesuit as interpreter, accompanied by forty soldiers. It was then transported quickly, in carts, to Peking, where the mission was confined to a courtyard guarded by soldiers. Five cooks and other servants were sent to them, and food and drink were supplied in sufficient quantities.[3]

After one week Milovanoff and his companions, were taken to the Office of the Ministry. One official asked them on what business they had come to see the Emperor. They answered, they came to China on

[1] Baddeley, op. cit., p. 196.

[2] Documents in Russian, No. 1, quoted in Chen, Yenching Journal of Social Studies, IV (Feb. 1949), 132.

[3] Baddeley, op. cit., pp. 198–199.

business stated in their official instructions. The official ordered them to read out the instructions, which was done by a clerk, and the interpreter repeated what they said while the Chinese secretary wrote it down. When this was completed, the official took the instructions in spite of Milovanoff's protest, and explained that it would be impossible to return them, because there would be a letter from the Emperor to the Csar.[1]

After another two weeks, Milovanoff and his companions were given an audience, in which they bowed down to the ground before the Emperor and then stood before him with their caps on while tea was served, after which the Emperor asked their ages. Later the Emperor gave them permission to go about Peking, and during two weeks they roamed at will through the city, with guards to take care of them. They took this opportunity to gather information about China, especially the commercial situation.[2]

After the mission had been in Peking for five weeks it was dismissed with honor and escorted back to the Naun River, where it was left in the care of governor Mangutei who was to escort it to Nerchinsk and turn over the Emperor's letter and the gifts to *voevoda* Arshinsky. Arshinsky reported to the Csar that the mission was treated by the Chinese Emperor with much honor, given plenty to eat and drink, and dismissed with many gifts.[3]

Arshinsky received the letter from the Chinese Emperor in Nerchinsk and ordered the interpreter to translate it, to the following effect:[4]

To the Great Lord Tsar and Grand Prince, Alexei Mikhailovich, autocrat of all the Russias, Great, Little, and White, from the Bogdoi Tsar this letter is (to say that) by this the Great Lord's command, Danilo Arshinsky had sent to him from Nerchinsk Fort as envoys, the Nerchinsk Cossacks, Ignashka Milovanoff and companions, to bring together by embassage Bogdoi Tsar and the Great Lord, and that people should go quietly, freely, and continually, for trade purposes, to and fro, and it was hoped that should there be any hostile approach from any outside quarters towards Nerchinsk Fort or to him, each should help the other, and as to Gantimur, Danilo Arshinsky had written to the Great Lord, and some of his, the Bogdoi Tsar's, hunters and trappers had been on the river Shilka sable hunting, and, coming back, they had stated that on the river Shilka in Albazin were dwelling some small number of Russians under Nikiforko Chernigoff, with Cossacks, who made war on his (i.e., the Bogdoi Khan's) extreme frontier people, the Dahurs and Chugars (?Djuchers). He, the Bogdoi Khan, had wished to send a military expedition against those Russians, but he was told that they were subjects of the Great Tsar, so he refrained from ordering them to be at-

[1] *Ibid.*, p. 199.
[2] *Ibid.*, pp. 199–202.
[3] *Ibid.*, pp. 202–203.
[4] *Ibid.*, pp. 196–197.

tacked, and sent (instead) his people to find out for certain whether it was subjects of the Tsar who lived in Nerchinsk; and from Nerchinsk, by order of the Great Lord, Danilo Arshinsky had sent them envoys with a letter. And now he, the Bogdoi Khan, had learnt for certain that in Nerchinsk Fort dwelt a *voevoda* and military people, subjects of the Great Lord; but in future let his extreme frontier people not be attacked nor any harm done to them, and let that promise be given and let them live in peace and in joy – that was why he, the Bogdoi Khan, had sent this letter to the Great Lord Tsar and Grand Prince, Alexei Mikhailovich, Autocrat of All Russias, Great, Little, and White.

The imperial letter shows that the Emperor was either ignorant of the Russian demands, or willfully ignoring them, and his statement to the Csar is in the usual commanding tone. The utter lack of mutual understanding, as demonstrated by the Russian demands and the Chinese reply, could hardly improve relations between the two countries. Milovanoff was made to bow down to the ground before the Emperor – a strange performance indeed, on the part of one who had come to demand the Emperor's acceptance of Russian suzerainty.

Since Gantimur was not surrendered the K'ang-hsi Emperor sent a letter to the Csar the following year, 1671. Verbiest's (a Jesuit) translation of the letter runs:[1]

Hoangti (the usual Chinese word for emperor) to thee Chagan Khan (White Khan): thy Danilo sent as a petition (to the effect) that thou also dost wish for friendship between us; he also writes regarding Gantimur that he has written to thee, and continues: 'I expect orders shortly and I will then send him on without delay, but let not the Djindji (or Nü-chi) who dwell not far from us do us any harm. Long since, our hunters sent a humble address declaring that those who dwell on the Black River (the Amur) are 'lovchi,'' petty robbers, in no great strength, but those 'lovchi' maltreat our Djindji and Takori (Dahurs), and catch their sables, and, withal, they humbly report of Gantimur that, relying on those 'lovchi' he has fled to them and trusts them. They petitioned therefore that those 'lovchi' should be punished. But I, Ruler of the World, hearing that those 'lovchi' were thy subjects, sent a man to find out what was true and what false. And that Danilo sent ten messengers with Ignatii (Milovanoff), and when they announced that they had thy authority and were subjects of thine, I believe them. But now, if thou desirest to live in peace, send us the refugee Gantimur. Also, in future, let none make any trouble on our frontiers, if this is done there will be peace; that is why I send this letter.

This letter was written in Manchu, and the Russians were unable to read it. The Csar did not reply, and the absence of a reply offended the K'ang-hsi Emperor, who refused to accept the Russian protestations of ignorance. Failure to reply caused many troubles for the Spathary mission which was to follow.

[1] *Ibid.*, pp. 372–373.

2. SPATHARY'S EMBASSY, 1675–1677

Despite the difficulties encountered by Russian missions to China, Russia never ceased to seek intercourse with China. The Spathary mission was dispatched with explicit instructions to establish diplomatic relations. He was instructed to find out whether in future there would be friendship and intercourse between the Csar and the Emperor, what was the safest trade route to China, and what the situation was in Siberia and China. He was also ordered to guard the style and title of the Csar vigilantly and to seek everywhere to put forward the Csar's name; and in all towns and other places to proclaim or praise it, and to speak in such manner as might serve to exalt both the name and honor of the Csar.[1]

With these instructions, Csar Alexei Mikhailovich, on February 20, 1675, appointed Nikolai Gavrilovich Spathary his ambassador, and bearer of his letter of greeting to the Chinese Emperor. With him Theodor Pavloff and Konstantine Grechanin were to proceed as dvorianins (nobles or noblemen) on the foreign list, and for secretarial work, Nikifor Veniukoff and Ivan Favoroff.[2] The ambassador and his suite set out from Moscow on March 3, and travelling by way of Pereslavl-zalieski, Rostoff, Yaroslavl, Vologda, Ustiung, Veliki, Soli Vui-chegotskoi, Kaigorodok, Soli Kameskoi, and the Siberian towns – Verk-hoturie, Turinskoi *Ostrog* and Tumen – reached Tobolsk on March 30, 1675.[3] From Tobolsk, to Spathary's knowledge, there were three ways to China: one was along the Irtish River and southern Mongolia, the route which Baikoff's mission took; the second was from Tobolsk to Selenga and thence through Urga to Peking; the third was from Tobolsk, through Yenisei and Selenga to Nerchinsk, and from thence via the Naun River and Manchuria to Peking.[4] Since the first two routes would probably be endangered by the war between Ochirtu and Galdan in the Mongol land, Spathary took the last way.[5] The mission arrived in Nerchinsk on December 4, 1675. Previously in July, Spathary, while sojourning in Yeniseik, sent Ignatii Milovanoff to China to announce the coming of the embassy. Milovanoff reached the

[1] *Ibid.*, p. 243.
[2] *Ibid.*, p. 242.
[3] *Ibid.*, pp. 242–243.
[4] *Ibid.*, p. 244.
[5] *Ibid.*, pp. 365–366.

Naun in December, and then set off to Peking, accompanied by Mangutei, the governor of the Naun.[1]

On December 19 the mission left Nerchinsk for Tsitsihar. After
crossing many rivers, such as the Shilka, Unda, Gaitimur (Kazimur),
Biurza, Argun, Khabur, Terbul, Han, Kailar, Dzadar, Unera, and
Uluchi, and many steppes, and finally the Targachun Range, they
reached the Naun River on January 23, 1676, and were received by
many Chinese officials before their arrival at the Naun (Tsitsihar).
On January 26, a Chinese official of rank came to meet Spathary, and
with him many Chinese people of honor, and five hundred soldiers. As
Chinese frontier officials, these people had orders to make inquiry of all
foreign folks as to whence they came, and what their business was,
friendly or otherwise – also to examine into everything closely, and
only in accordance with the result of such inquiry could they dare to
furnish food and conveyances. To these questions Spathary replied
that the Russian Csar, desiring to maintain neighborly relations and
friendship with the Chinese Emperor, had sent him to the latter, and
that his particular business would be evident to the Emperor himself
when the ambassador reached the Emperor's presence. The Chinese
officials demanded more information and ultimately Spathary produced
a letter of the Chinese Emperor which they themselves had sent some
years before, through Nerchinsk, to the Russian Csar. No sooner had
they caught sight of the letter than they recognized it, and without
reading it, declared that they now believed Spathary was sent by the
Russian Csar on a state mission. They immediately gave orders to
establish the mission near their settlement, and supplied food at a
definite rate, until a delegation arrived from Peking with Mangutei, the
governor of Naun, and Milovanoff, who had gone in advance to Peking
to report the coming of the Russian embassy.[2]

While Spathary and his suite lived with these frontier officials, they
talked about the letter which Spathary had shown the Chinese. The
Chinese officials asserted that in the letter the Emperor had demanded
that the Csar surrender the deserter Gantimur, and asked whether
Russia would surrender him. Spathary replied that the Csar was in
ignorance of the contents of the letter, and for his part he told them
that Gantimur and his tribe had already come under the jurisdiction of
Russia. The Chinese officials also complained that the Russian Cossacks
in Albazin had taken tribute from a certain Tungus princeling,

[1] *Ibid.*, p. 276.
[2] *Ibid.*, pp. 286–289.

Petrushka, who dwelt on the Lena. Spathary gave the same answer that Petrushka was under Russian jurisdiction.[1] The conversations indicated the difficulties involved in Sino-Russian relations at that time.

Real troubles began after Milovanoff and governor Mangutei, and later the *Askaniama* Ma-la, (*Askaniama* was presumably Shih-lang or vice president of board) arrived from Peking on February 18 and February 26, respectively; the *Askaniama* was sent by the Emperor to meet the embassy. Ma-la insisted that Spathary should visit him first, but Spathary refused on the ground of sovereign equality. The argument went on for several days, but at length the *Askaniama* gave in a little; they met in a tent wherever Spathary chose to set it up. Spathary entered it first, and the *Askaniama* came afterwards. The *Askaniama* said that he had been dispatched with the most stringent injunctions to take from Spathary the Csar's letter and open it and read it, to see what it contained; further, that he must make strict inquiry as to all other matters, and send word to the Emperor immediately. If Spathary refused to deliver up the Csar's letter and make no answers as to certain other matters, he was to be treated as Theodor Baikoff. He had special orders to find out what answer was given by the Csar concerning the surrender of Gantimur.

Spathary, however, positively refused to deliver the Csar's letter to the *Askaniama*, because it seemed to him that his credentials could only be presented to the sovereign himself according to diplomatic usage. However, according to Chinese practice a letter sent by a foreign sovereign to the Chinese Emperor should be opened and examined by frontier officials to make sure that the style and expressions were correct, and if they were not, it should be corrected on the frontier so as not to insult the Emperor. Different customs as to procedure produced difficulties in this case. As to the surrender of Gantimur, Spathary repeated that owing to ignorance of the language, the Csar did not know anything about the content of the letter relating to Gantimur. *Askaniama* did not believe that the Csar lacked knowledge of the matter, and he suspected the sincerity of Russia's desire to have friendship with China.[2] The difference of customs between Russia and China and the difficulty of language aggravated the suspicion of both the *Askaniama* and Spathary.

Their arguments went on for a month with little progress, but in the

[1] *Ibid.*, pp. 290–291.
[2] *Ibid.*, pp. 293–312.

end each made concessions. Spathary told the *Askaniama* what the Csar's letter contained; and the latter recorded the former's words. Also the *Askaniama* wrote out all the conversations they had had, and these written minutes were sent to the Chinese Emperor for decision. On April 13, 1676, the *Askaniama*, in good spirits, visited Spathary to announce that the Emperor, wishing that friendship and love be confirmed between the two countries, had sent orders to bring Spathary's mission, numbering one hundred fifty men, to Peking, showing them all honor. On April 17, 1676, the *Askaniama* and the ambassador with their suites started from the Naun River. They traveled southwestward, through the provinces of Heilungkiang, Kirin, Liaoning, and Jehol, and entered China proper by the Hsi-fen Pass of the Great Wall, and reached Peking on May 16, 1676. Spathary and his suite were brought to a compound not far from the city, where they were lodged. The courtyard was spacious, but the buildings were old and many of them in ruins. In the compound various other envoys had already been lodged, such as the Dutch and Portuguese. All envoys lodged there were supplied food by the Chinese government.[1]

No sooner had the mission settled down than the quarrel over the delivery of the Csar's letter was resumed. The *Askaniama* explained that the letter should in no case be presented to the Emperor directly. If the ambassador was unwilling to give it up to the *Askaniama*, he must at least give it to the board. He insisted that if the Emperor received the ambassador in person, all the sovereigns of neighboring states would leave off calling him Emperor. If the Emperor, contrary to custom, took the Csar's letter himself, he would suffer much dishonor. But Spathary still was resolutely obstinate. On June 2, owing to the desire of both sides to establish friendly relations, an agreement was worked out. Ambassador Spathary, regardless of the Emperor's presence, was to surrender the Csar's letter to the Grand Secretaries (Kolai), and he was to prepare three versions of the letter to facilitate understanding it. Spathary refused to give up the presents in advance and insisted that they and the letter must go together. He also refused to "kotow" or to discuss the question until he saw what respect was to be shown to the Csar's letter.

On June 4, the *Askaniama* came to announce the Emperor's decision as follows: the Chinese Emperor, honoring the Russian Csar's majesty above all other sovereigns, and his embassy beyond all others that had ever been received, had commanded to have a place prepared within

---

[1] *Ibid.*, pp. 313–326.

the Forbidden City; at that place would be gathered the mandarins and most intimate counsellors; and the next day, at the first hour, horses would be sent and all the Csar's gifts would be put on little tables which would be carried before the ambassador; after that all three versions of the Csar's letter would be carried; and when he reached the Forbidden City, a place would be ready for Spathary facing the Emperor's throne; and there he should set down the letters and the gifts would be set close by. After the ambassador handed over the Csar's letter and gifts to the Grand Secretaries without a word, he should go back to his lodging. Also upon reaching the Emperor's court, he was to dismount at a column, on which the Emperor's name was inscribed; and the ambassador and his suite were to go on foot to the court.[1] Spathary deemed that such an arrangement would guard the honor of the Csar, and accepted it. Actually, the proposal did no greater honor to Russia, for Spathary was only to be received among many others at an ordinary early court gathering.

On June 5, Spathary went to the Chinese Emperor's court, and in accordance with the previous arrangement, delivered the letters and gifts to the chief Grand Councillor and departed without a word. On June 8 some people of the Chinese court came to the ambassador and asked if he had any message to give. Spathary, with the aid of a Jesuit interpreter, prepared a statement containing the twelve following requests (no version of the original letter can be found): (1) that several earlier Chinese letters carried by Spathary be translated; (2) that a language be agreed upon for future use, both for letters and references; (3) that, on both sides, the names and titles of the Csar and the Emperor should be written in accordance with model letters (to be agreed upon); (4) that the Emperor should send an ambassador back with him; (5) that merchants be allowed to go to and fro freely, on either side; (6) that Russian prisoners, if any, be set free; (7) that each year forty thousand pounds (Russian) of silver be sent from China to the Muscovite Kingdom in exchange for such Russian goods as they may want; (8) that precious stones should also be sent to Russia in exchange for goods; (9) that some bridge builders be lent to Russia; (10) that Russians be permitted to buy what they wished with goods sent from Russia and that fixed customs duty be levied; (11) that the shortest and most convenient trade route be established – preferably by sea and by rivers – and that the embassy be sent back that way; (12) that these requests

---

[1] *Ibid.*, pp. 330–352.

be accepted in love and friendship, for it was the ambassador's desire that the Csar and Emperor should always dwell thus.[1]

Pleased by the Russian royal letter and gifts, the Emperor deigned to give an official audience to Spathary. A long controversy developed over the question of the kotow, which Spathary first refused to perform, but later agreed to do in return for additional honors, because he feared that his whole mission would be ruined, if he did not consent to it. On June 15, the ambassador and his immediate suite were given an audience in the Tsu-Kuang-ko, or "pavilion of purple light," where the Mongol princes always performed homage. At that pavilion they observed many mandarins performing the "kotow" before the Emperor's throne in the Great Hall for their own benefit, so that they in turn should know what to do. The two mandarins attending the ambassador told the Jesuit interpreter that the time had come for the ambassador to go and kotow. They came to the Great Hall and halted and the two mandarins and the Jesuit stood aside. The music played, the bell rang out, the drum sounded; and a man cried out "bow down!" and the ambassador began bowing quickly and not to the ground, so that the officials told the Jesuit to tell him he must bow down to the ground and less quickly, as the mandarins had done. After kotowing, he was brought to the inner hall where the Emperor was sitting. When he reached there, he was told to bow to the ground once, after which he sat down on a cloth cushion where he could see the Emperor quite well. After tea was served, the ambassador and his suite were dismissed and they returned to the embassy compound.[2]

After this audience, discussion about some of the ambassador's requests began. First of all, the *Askaniama* came to talk with Spathary about translating the letters. The letters were first copied and later interpreted. Two of them were very old, having been written by the Ming Emperor Yung-lo. They had not been addressed to the Csar, but were letters of grace to certain mandarins dwelling on the Amur. The other two letters were in Manchu; the most recent one was concerned with the surrender of the deserter Gantimur, and had been given to Milovanoff in 1670. The older one was from the Shun-chih Emperor to the Csar on the occasion of the Perlifieff mission of 1658–62, and stated in an arrogant way that the tribute sent by the Csar had been accepted, and that the Emperor sent the Csar in return grace and gifts.

The topic of trade was taken up next. Since the Russians had brought

[1] *Ibid.*, pp. 352–353.
[2] *Ibid.*, pp. 353–361.

merchandise to sell, the *Askaniama* said that the Emperor had given orders for the gates of the compound to be opened so that traders might come in to buy and sell. Lists were to be made of all the merchandise, distinguishing between that belonging to the Csar's treasury and that belonging to the Cossacks. Thus the Russians were allowed to display their goods to the Chinese merchants in the compound, but were not allowed to go around to the city to buy and sell, because they came as an embassy, not as ordinary merchants. The embassy was strictly guarded by Chinese soldiers.[1] This was to protect the embassy and was considered a great honor to the ambassador and it also served to prevent any trouble and quarrels arising from the conduct of people, but the ambassador complained of the prisonlike arrangement.

A major point of discussion was the release of Russian prisoners which involved a great deal of contention. Russia demanded that Russian prisoners of war should be surrendered without ransom or exchanged, and that traitors should be surrendered without ransom. The Chinese demanded that Chinese deserters, especially Gantimur, to the Russian side should be sent back to China. Both sides ultimately agreed that, for the enhancement of friensdhip, mutual surrender of fugitives was necessary.[2]

On July 8 the Emperor gave a dinner for Spathary and his suite, at which they kotowed and prostrated themselves. At the dinner the *Askaniama* talked over various matters including the purchase of the Russian goods and the sale of Chinese goods. Some days later, the *Askaniama* and Spathary again took up the subject of trade. From China's point of view it had sufficient goods for its people and it did not need foreign goods in large amount, but for the benefit of both sides, trade might serve as a tie of friendship. China, therefore, encouraged the establishment of intercourse between the two countries, but it was the ancient custom, however, that envoys and merchants be treated in a different way. Merchants were given only seven weeks time, after which they were sent packing, whether they had sold their goods or not. However, they were free to come or not as they liked, whereas an ambassador was kept within gates. Spathary had come to China as ambassador, and yet he also wanted to be a merchant; this was not allowed, according to Chinese custom. Therefore the dispute lasted long.[3]

[1] *Ibid.*, pp. 361–363, 365.
[2] *Ibid.*, pp. 366–367.
[3] *Ibid.*, pp. 378–384.

On July 19 the ambassador and his suite were summoned to audience again. They were accompanied into the Great Hall by the *Alikhamba* (*Shang-shu* or president of board), the *Askaniama*, and a Jesuit, Alikhakhava (presumably Verbiest), as interpreter, where they bowed to the Emperor as before, going down nine times on their knees and bowing their heads each time. Spathary was ordered by the Emperor to sit near the throne. The *Alikhamba* placed the ambassador's red cushion for him, and, having done so, bade him prostrate himself once, and after that sit down. His suite prostrated themselves in the same way but were seated behind the ambassador. Then the Grand Secretary, who formerly took over the Csar's letter, and two Jesuits came to the Emperor; and they fell on their knees, and the Emperor spoke to them softly. After that all three came to the ambassador and, speaking in the same low tone, told him to fall on his knees, when the Jesuit Alikhakhava said:

> The great Autocrat of the whole Chinese Empire, the Khan, asks if His Majesty the Autocrat of all the Russias is in good health?

And the ambassador answered:

> By the grace of God, the Great Lord Tsar and Grand Prince Alexei Mikhailovich, Autocrat of All Russias, Great, Little, and White, when we left His Majesty the Great Lord in his mighty and famous kingdom, was in good health and reigning happily; and His Majesty the Great Lord Tsar wished your majesty, the Bogdik-han, likewise many years of good health and successful sovereignty, as his most dear neighbor and friend.

Then all three returned together to the Emperor and fell again on their knees. They came again to the ambassador and said:

> The Great Khan asks three questions: how old is His Majesty the Tsar? How tall is he? And how long ago did he begin to reign?

The ambassador answered each question clearly. Then there were some questions about the ambassador himself, and he also answered in a good manner. After the inquiry the dinner was served. The Emperor ordered the first cup of wine, which was made of grapes, to be offered to the ambassador. So the *Alikhamba* and the Jesuit came to him and told him about it, and he took the cup, and holding it in his left hand, put his right hand to the ground and drank. When the ambassador had finished drinking, he bowed again and then sat down in his place. When the dinner was over, the ambassador and his suite were dismissed to the embassy compound.[1]

---

[1] *Ibid.*, pp. 385–388.

Later the Jesuit secretly came to tell the ambassador the intention of the Chinese Emperor. He said that if the Csar did not surrender the deserter Gantimur, China would go to war with Russia. The Emperor meant also to capture the frontier forts of Albazin and Nerchinsk, because the Russians had become formidable in their eyes, especially since they had learnt that the Russians were there by the Csar's orders. They knew that at present the garrisons in those places were not numerous and that Moscow was far away, and their plan was to wait until the number of their own troops on the frontier was augmented; and they cared less about getting hold of Gantimur than about finding out what were the Csar's intentions. If the Csar gave up Gantimur, who was the chieftain of many native people, the rest of them would follow him, or scatter in various directions, so that it would no longer be worth the Csar's while to spend money in maintaining troops on the Amur. The Jesuit thought the Chinese would await one more reply from the Csar, after the ambassador's return, before attacking, provided the border Cossacks committed no breach of the peace. If, however, it were the Csar's intention to refuse to give over Gantimur, troops in large numbers should be sent without delay to defend those forts.[1]

China took the position that no diplomatic relations between the two countries could be established before Russia surrendered Gantimur and stopped the Cossacks invasion of the Amur. Until the Csar gave a positive answer to these questions prolonged parleys were useless. Moreover, the Cossacks attached to the mission beat the guards who were on duty in the embassy compound and wandered around the city in contradiction to Chinese order. Such actions made the Chinese government more unpleasant and speeded the dismissal of the embassy.

In August the ambassador was summoned to receive the Emperor's gifts to the Csar, but he refused to kotow when receiving them. This aggravated the unpleasant situation. On August 29, the ambassador and his suite were summoned to the Forbidden City to receive the Emperor's letter to the Csar. Outside the city gate where the Csar's letter had been received, he was told to sit down. At the gate stood two Grand Secretaries, the former one, and an old Chinese, also the *Alik-hamba* – for the *Askaniama* at that time was unwell – and with him was the Jesuit. When the ambassador drew near, one of the Grand Secretaries said that he and all those with him must fall on their knees to hear the Emperor's decree. They did so and the Grand Secretary began

---

[1] *Ibid.*, p. 395.

to speak in the Chinese tongue, the *Alikhamba* repeating what he said
in Mongol to the Russian interpreter, saying:[1]

The Khan does not choose to write any answer to the Tsar for two reasons:
first, because you have been disobedient, refusing to accept the gifts for your
sovereign lord on your knees, as do the envoys of other neighboring monarchs;
nor indeed does anyone dare to impugn that custom. Secondly, even if the
Khan deigned to write to the Tsar, his only real object is to have Gantimur sent
here; and that was stated in the former letter. As the Tsar has not sent Gantimur
back, the Khan will not write again; nor until that matter is settled, can anything else be entered upon. For Danilo Arshinsky sent people here asking His
Majesty the Khan that his subjects should keep peace on the border, promising,
as to Gantimur, that he would write to the Tsar, who would, of course, give
him up. Yet Gantimur has not been surrendered, nor is there peace on the border.
There is therefore nothing to write about. More than that – in future, we will
have neither letters, nor ambassadors, nor envoys, nor merchants from the land
of the Tsar so long as these three demands remain unsatisfied: first, that Gantimur be sent here accompanied by your ambassador; secondly, that that ambassador be a most reasonable man who will do all we command him, in accordance
with our customs, and oppose us in nothing; thirdly, that at all frontier places,
inhabited by any of your Sovereign Lord's border people, the peace be kept
unbroken.

After hearing the Emperor's decree, the ambassador argued that the
refusal to take the gifts on his knees only safeguarded the Csar's honor
and that, as to Gantimur, the Csar knew nothing about what the
Emperor had written in his letter. Also he asked the Chinese to reply
to the requests which the ambassador had made. These arguments
resulted in nothing, and the Chinese still insisted that Russia should
fulfill the three demands as prerequisites to further intercourse. The
Chinese officials went on to explain their customs in detail.

Some days later they talked about the style and title of future address between the two sovereigns. In this talk the Chinese stated three
things: (1) when the Emperor writes an answer to any other sovereign,
he frames it as from the Most Exalted Throne to an inferior place; (2)
Russian presents to China would be accepted as tribute (or *yasak*); (3)
gifts sent by China to Russia are a gratuity for services rendered.

Spathary disagreed very much, saying that it was a marvellous
thing that when the Csar sent gifts to the Emperor out of love and
friendship, China called them tribute, as though the Csar were the
Emperor's subject, whereas all the world knew that the Csar, though
he took tribute from many, paid it to none. The ambassador was
dissatisfied with this whole turn of events because it was his intention
to get the Csar and the Emperor on an equal footing.[2]

[1] *Ibid.*, pp. 403–404.
[2] *Ibid.*, pp. 404–408.

The Grand Secretary declared that, at the end of the Csar's letter to the Emperor, the Csar wrote:[1]

Be not surprised if we write not your name and title in due form, for we are in ignorance; and in future we will write both name and title according to your dignity, as you yourself do.

This showed, he argued, that the Csar commanded the ambassador to conform to the Chinese customs and accept whatever letter the Emperor might write, and that the ambassador should, therefore, not refuse to accept what the Chinese demanded.

Spathary again made effort to obtain an equal footing for the Csar, but the Grand Secretary said that it was impossible for China to waive its long established custom, and hinting that the ambassador must make ready for the road. On September 1, 1676, the Emperor ordered the Russian embassy to leave Peking that very day. The *Alikhamba* came to the embassy courtyard to announce the dismissal, and repeated the three demands set forth in the Emperor's decree. He stated that if the Csar complied with these three demands, then the Emperor would look with favor upon the requests made by the ambassador, but until the three demands were fulfilled no Russian emissaries or traders were to come to China. Spathary requested delay of departure for another day, because of the sudden order and the muddy road. The *Alikhamba* replied that the order must be fulfilled at once, and that they must start for T'ung-chou by evening.[2]

The embassy complied with the order and left Peking after four o'clock in the afternoon, and reached T'ung-chou by midnight. It returned to Nerchinsk by the route it had come, accompanied by the *Askaniama*, Ma-la, and the governor of the Naun, Mangutei. On the way, the Chinese officials talked again with Spathary concerning the exchange of deserters and the maintenance of border peace. The Chinese stated that if the Csar would surrender Gantimur, China would return the Yakuts who had fled from the Lena area. In accordance with the Csar's order the ambassador should write to the Albazin Cossacks to keep the peace, and the Chinese in return should impress on their subjects that they must not interfere with either the Russians or their tributary nations when they went hunting. Mangutei, after adding that the Russians must in no case come to the Naun, whether for trade or other purposes, agreed to keep the peace on the frontier.

---

[1] *Ibid.*, p. 409.
[2] *Ibid.*, pp. 410–414.

This amounted to a local arrangement to keep peace on the border.[1]

The Chinese recorded the coming of this mission in a very succinct way. We paraphrase the records here as a summary of the description of the mission and also to show the Chinese attitude toward the mission. In the fifth month of the fifteenth year of K'ang-hsi, i.e., June, 1676, the Russian Csar dispatched Ambassador Nikolai Gavrilovich Spathary to pay tribute to China. His credential letter stated that, being situated far away, Russia had never had intercourse with China from the earliest times. Because of ignorance of the Chinese language, letter style, and court etiquette, the Csar himself felt incomplete in expressing his sincerity toward the Chinese Emperor. Now he vigilantly has sent an envoy to beg pardon and pay tribute to the Emperor. The Emperor issued a decree to permit the payment of tribute.[2] These records clearly indicate that China considered the mission as no more than a tribute embassy, although Spathary was dispatched by the Csar to China as an extraordinary ambassador.

During the negotiation, China claimed the extradition of the deserter Gantimur and the withdrawal of Russia from Albazin. Spathary, on the other hand, demanded establishment of commercial and diplomatic relations. These were the real purposes of the negotiation on the part of each side. However, before the real subjects could be taken up the negotiations were stalled by the problems of etiquette. As a result, the mission failed.

As a matter of fact, the main cause for the failure of the mission was the border disputes on the Amur, of which the Gantimur case was a striking illustration, because the Russian action in this matter proved, to the mind of the Chinese, that Russia had no good intention toward China. Moreover, since Russia was far away, the Chinese thought it would be difficult for Russia to send a large army to the Amur, and at that time, Russia had an insufficient number of troops on the Amur to do the Chinese any harm. On the other hand, the natives around the Amur River belonged to the same race as the Manchus and were most likely to give allegiance to China; and, more important, China had a fairly strong force on the Amur and had already defeated the Russians several times. Thus China had a better power position on the Amur than Russia, and, under the circumstances, did not feel it necessary to deal with Russia as an equal. That is why the Chinese officials took an

[1] *Ibid.*, pp. 415–420.
[2] *Chin-tin huang-chao wen-hsien tung-kao,* in So-fang pei-ch'eng, preli. Chüan XI, pp. 5b6a. *Ching shih lu,* K'ang-hsi, Chüan LXI, pp. 3b4a. *Tung hua lu,* Chüan XVII, p. 15a.

arrogant attitude toward the Spathary's embassy and compelled it to leave in an unceremonious manner. The difference of customs and the difficulty of language also contributed to the failure of the mission. For example, China according to its custom treated merchants and envoys differently; and envoys should not carry on commercial transactions. But Spathary claimed the privileges and conveniences both of an envoy and of a merchant which the Chinese would not allow. On the other hand, the Manchu rulers were campaigning against the Sanfan rebellion in south China, and did not wish to precipitate difficulties on their northern frontier at that time. For this reason China did render some honor to Spathary and his master, the Csar, which had not been shared by other envoys and sovereigns.

CHAPTER VIII

SINO-RUSSIAN WAR ON THE AMUR

I. GROWING TENSION ON THE AMUR, 1676–1684

As stated earlier the Russians reappeared on the Amur owing to the withdrawal of the Chinese from Albazin and to the greedy expansion of Russia toward the Amur. Although Spathary had directed that the Russians were not to navigate the lower Amur and Dzeya nor collect tribute from the Tunguzians, his directions were disregarded. In 1676 a Yashnoi Simovie was built at the mouth of the Gilui from whence parties went to the upper Dzeya to collect tribute. In 1678 Zeisko *ostrog* was built at the mouth of the Numisha (Amumish), and many tribesmen were forced to pay tribute to Albazin. In 1679 Selimbinskoi *ostrog* was built on the Slimba and Dolonskoi *ostrog* on the Dolonza. In 1681, the Russians built an *ostrog* on the Arguni, the first one, in that region. In the same year, several *ostrogs* were built on the Dzeya and its branches, interfering greatly with Chinese hunters and traders. China remonstrated but was loath to act. In 1683 a Russian party from Albazin found on the Bureya River, twenty Chinese hunters and traders burnt them alive in their huts, and carried away whatever property they had. Moreover, many Chinese criminals fled to Albazin where they were protected. It also became difficult at times for China to gather tribute from certain native tribes who tried to play off one government against the other. These matters irritated China and finally drove her to take up arms.[1]

The Solons – the Dauris and Ducheris – on the Amur and Sungari belong to the same race as the Manchu, and had been Manchu tributaries for a long time. They were immediate neighbors of the Manchus, who had long considered these people as their own. The Russian invasion was, without doubt, an encroachment on the original place of

[1] Golder, *op. cit.*, p. 56.

Manchu power.[1] After the able K'ang-hsi Emperor had consolidated power in China, he would no longer tolerate the Russian advance on the Amur.

War between China and Russia seemed inevitable. However before going to war China tried by peaceful means to persuade the Cossacks to give up the Chinese outlaws, to be more merciful to the natives, and either to go back to Russia or to accept asylum in China. Twice, in 1681 and 1682, China sent messengers to Nerchinsk asking for a conference. At the same time a letter was dispatched to Albazin, complaining of Russian cruelty to the natives and asking the Russians to withdraw to their own country. Whenever Russians fell into their hands, the Chinese invariably treated them kindly and sent them back, sometimes with letters to their own people. But neither these acts of goodness nor the entreaties, nor the letters to Moscow succeeded in bringing satisfactory results. The inhabitants of Albazin not only did not fear the *voevoda* at Nerchinsk, but they openly defied and threatened him. Realizing that words were to no purpose, China prepared to act.[2]

As soon as the Sanfan rebellion was put down in south China, the K'ang-hsi Emperor started preparation on a large scale for war on the Amur. As an experienced soldier he fully appreciated the fighting ability of his adversaries, and accordingly he planned with methodical care and thoroughness. In order not to repeat the mistakes of the battle of Khumarsk in 1655, special attention was paid to the supply of provisions and the maintenance of communications. In 1680, a number of transports were constructed for use on the Manchurian waterways, the rivers Liao, Itung, Sungari and Amur. Meanwhile, to insure the supply of provisions, granaries were established along the Itung, and the system of military farming was introduced in Aigun. Rice exports from Manchuria were prohibited.[3]

Two lines of communications were established, one by water the other by land. In 1682 the Emperor sent Lieutenant-generals Lang Tan and P'eng Ch'ung to the land of the Dahurs and Solons in the vicinity of Albazin, ostensibly on a reindeer hunting trip, but in reality to reconnoiter the Russian situation.[4] Lang Tan was personally instructed by the Emperor to investigate the water route from Ninguta through

---

[1] *Ping-tin lu-cha fang lüeh*, in So-fang pei-ch'eng, prel. Chüan VI, p. 17a.
[2] Golder, *op. cit.*, p. 57.
[3] Chen, *Yenching Journal of Social Studies*, IV (February, 1949), 123.
[4] *So-fang pei-ch'eng*, preli. Chüan V, p. 1b. "Lang Tan Lieh-Chüan (Lang Tan's Biography)," in Chao Erh-hsün, *Ching Shih Kao* (Draft History of the Ching Dynasty), (Hong Kong: Wen-hsüeh Yen-Chin Shê, 1960), II, 1100.

the Ussuri to the Amur. In 1683 another party headed by Galtu was sent to measure the depth of the river bed of the Liao, and the information thus acquired was utilized in the building of a canal connecting that river with the Sungari. Three years later, nineteen postal stations were set up between Kirin and Aigun.[1]

As far as military preparations were concerned, emphasis was laid both on land and naval warfare. In 1682 the Emperor sent the finance minister, Yishongna to Ninguta to supervise the construction of warships. In the same year Bahai and his forces were ordered to be stationed in Aigun and Khumarsk. Also China ordered Norbu, a tribe of Tsetsen Khan, to sever trade with the Russians at Nerchinsk, hoping that the Russians would suffer from such an economic boycott.[2] Previously in 1676 the headquarters of the Special Defense Commissioner of Ninguta was moved to Kirin, a point more strategically located for the Amur campaign; in 1683, another new office, the military governor of Heilungkiang, was created, with headquarters at Aigun, where the Dzeya flows into the Amur. In order to train a navy, a dockyard was built in Kirin. Many warships were built, and several thousand sailors were recruited from among the exiles from the maritime province of south China.[3]

Meanwhile, Lang Tan returned from his reconnoitering expedition. He recommended that a contingent of three thousand men would suffice in an offensive against the Locha. This recommendation was accepted by the Emperor, who, a military perfectionist, yet peacefully inclined, expressed his feeling thus:[4]

We would prefer not to commence hostilities, for war is a great misfortune. For the present we order one-thousand five-hundred troops to be collected in Kirin and Ninguta. Warships to be built, and cannon and guns to be prepared, so that the men may be trained. At Aigun and Khumarsk, wooden fortifications should be built opposite the Russian ostrogs on the other bank of the river. The supply of provisions should come from the government farms of the Kortsins and Sibe and in Kirin. Here twelve thousand shih (one shih is the equivalent of about 140 pounds) of millet should be available and should suffice for three years.

The preparations – intelligence, provisions, communications, ammunition, and men – took three full years of planning and execution. When all was completed, K'ang-hsi still made another attempt to settle the Locha controversy without bloodshed. In the spring of 1682, an

[1] Chen, *Yenching Journal of Social Studies*, IV (February, 1949), 124.
[2] *Ibid.*
[3] *Ibid.*, pp. 24–25.
[4] *Ping-ting lo-cha fang-lüeh*, in *So-fang pei-ch'eng*, prel. Chüan V, p. 5a, quoted in Chen, *Yenching Journal of Social Studies*, IV (February, 1949), 125.

edict was sent to the Russian governor of Albazin. It began by making known China's grievances against the Russians. "You have broken into our country and driven out our subjects and destroyed their sable trade. You have received Gantimur and his comrades among you and inspired revolutions along our frontiers." It then urged them "to give up your bad intentions, to forsake our territory and give up our Gantimur." Should the Russian fail to comply, the Emperor threatened to send his forces against them. Meanwhile, however, he promised them "an honorable treatment and recompense." [1] Thirty Cossacks on the Amur, who had been captured, were treated with hospitality. Of these the Emperor now selected two as bearers of his edict to Albazin, requesting the governor to send back his answer through them and to come himself to Peking, or to send a delegate.[2]

To K'ang-hsi's offer the Russians gave no reply. Order was therefore given to the Chinese army to start campaign. The Russians received the first authentic news of the Chinese army under the command of Sapusu in 1683 when 67 Albazin Cossacks ran into a Chinese force on the Dureya River. A number of Russians were taken prisoners. The Emperor ordered not to kill them but to treat them kindly. Tempting offers were made to them to enlist in the Chinese army where a number of other Russians were already serving. On the Dzeya and below it forts were erected to prevent the Russians from going down the river.[3] At the close of 1683 all of the Russians settlements on the lower Amur and its tributaries had been destroyed and Albazin alone remained. Early in 1684 Sapusu and his army of three thousand men equipped with armor were ordered to induce the surrender of the Cossacks and to stop grain supplies to starve them. In the meantime, two Russian prisoners were sent with a letter to the leader of the Cossacks at Albazin. In it promises and threats were used to induce the garrison to surrender, but they failed in their effect. All Cossacks declared in favor of defending the place. Thus comes the major war in 1685.[4]

---

[1] *Tung hua lu*, K'ang-hsi, Chüan XXXII, p. 31ab, edict to Li-fan Yuan, quoted in Chen, *Yenching Journal of Social Studies*, IV (February, 1949), 125.

[2] John Dudgeon, *Historical Sketch of the Ecclesiastical, Political and Commercial Relations of Russia with China*, Peking, 1872, Pt. II, p. 2, quoted in Chen, *Yenching Journal of Social Studies*, IV (February, 1949), 121–126.

[3] Golder, *op. cit.*, p. 58.

[4] Ravenstein, *op. cit.*, p. 46.

2. THE ALBAZIN WAR, 1685–1686

Early in 1685 the Chinese advanced towards Albazin and surrounded the place. A new governor of Albazin called Alexei Tolbuzin, made efforts to resist the Chinese attack but the resources of about 450 men, including hunters, merchants, farmers and Cossacks left at his disposal were insufficient to resist a prolonged seige. The Chinese forces ascending the Amur by water and land, according to the Russians, numbered about eighteen thousand men equipped with guns and cannons.[1] The Russian records are exaggerations. The Chinese official records state that fifteen hundred were sent to Aigun. These were presently reinforced by four hundred armed with cane shields from the province of Fukien and five hundred more from other places. In addition one thousand artillery men were recruited from four provinces.[2] Even if all Chinese forces had been present at Albazin, the total could not have exceeded 3,400. All Chinese forces were put under the command of General P'eng Ch'ung. No sooner had his army appeared before Albazin on June 13, 1685, than he proclaimed the K'ang-hsi's edict as follows to the Russians, which was translated into Manchu, Polish and Russian:[3]

Many times have I sent message to you that you should withdraw all men on the Amur and return all the deserters. Many years have you penetrated into the interior, abducted women and disturbed order. Thereby, I dispatch forces to cut your return route, for the purpose of forcing the surrender of the Locha at Hunkung and other places. They will be pardoned and will not be killed. Because you still remained in Yaksa (Albazin), I have to send a strong expedition to attack you. By such strong forces you will be easily exterminated. But I always take pity on all people in my land. Desiring then, to have security, I am not willing to exterminate them immediately. I have made my intention known again and again. If you want peace, you must return to Yakutsk at once, as the boundary for hunting and collecting tribute. You must not intrude into my land to disturb order. If you extradite to me the deserters, and I will extradite Locha deserters to you in return. If all this is done, trade can still be carried on on the frontier. No war will be constituted and peace will be maintained. If still you are blind to my order, my forces will seize Yaksa and all of you will be exterminated.

Here we are made aware of the Chinese intention that the Yakutsk area should be regarded as the boundary, and, if the Russians withdrew, then trade could be carried on in the frontier territory. However, the

---

[1] *Ibid.*, p. 47.
[2] *So-fang pei-ch'eng*, preli. Chüan II, p. 2ab.
[3] *P'ing-ting lo-cha fang-lüeh*, in *So-fang pei-ch'eng*, preli. Chüan II, p. 10ab.

Russians at Albazin made no answer. P'eng Ch'ung started attacking Albazin at dawn on June 26, 1885, (25th day of the fifth month of the twenty fourth year of K'ang-hsi), after heavy arms had been properly placed. Ultimately the chief of the Locha, Alexei Tolbusin, in view of the pressing situation, came before the Chinese forces and bowed down to beg to surrender. Accordingly, P'eng Ch'ung declared the virtue of the Emperor in not wishing people to die, and released the Locha mass. Their deputy chief Pasheli and forty persons did not want to go back to Russia and were permitted to remain in the Chinese encampment. All Mongol and Solon deserters and prisoners were assembled. Yaksa was thus recovered.[1]

The Russian account of the war is generally similar but adds some details. After several charges, the Russians suffered a great deal. The Albazin priest Yermaghar, considering the situation a hopeless one, entreated Tolbuzin to declare a truce. Tolbusin acceded to the request and a deputation was sent to the Chinese general and the terms of surrender were arranged. The garrison was permitted to retreat to Nerchinsk with its arms and baggage, but twenty five who preferred to go over to the Chinese were permitted to do so. While returning the garrison met reinforcements. Had the reinforcements come a day earlier, the fall of Albazin might have been averted. As it was, all returned to Nerchinsk.

The Chinese followed the retreating Russians at a distance as far as the river Argun. On their return to Albazin they burned the fort and dwelling houses but left the fields untouched. They then retired down the Amur to Aigun. This was a big blunder on the part of the Chinese. If the Chinese had left an army in Albazin and fortified the place, the Russians would not have been able to recover it and the further troubles would have been forestalled. Russia, having heard the fall of Albazin, instructed the *voevoda* at Nerchinsk, Ivan Blassof, to take under his jurisdiction the men of Albazin and the government property and to send Tolbusin to Yenisei. All this shows that the intention of the Russian government was to abandon the post. But before these orders arrived the Cossacks had taken matters into their own hands. On July 10, soon after reaching Nerchinsk, Tolbusin and his men petitioned to be allowed to go back to gather the harvest of grain. The *voevoda* of Nerchinsk gave the permission and ordered them to reconnoiter the vicinity of the deserted fortress. On their return they reported that the Chinese had deserted Albazin and retired to Aigun,

---

[1] *Ibid.*, p. 16.

and that the grain had not been disturbed. Under the circumstances, the Nerchinsk *voevoda*, without loss of time, despatched Beiton with two hundred men to Albazin. Beiton's regiment had just arrived at Nerchinsk from Siberia before the fall of Albazin. He was followed by Tolbusin, who at the request of the former inhabitants, was again appointed governor. They at once set about gathering in the harvest, and after they had harvested the crop they built a new Albazin on the ruins of the old one. During the winter all hands were kept busy erecting fortifications under the able direction of Beiton, to whom great credit is due for the defense of the *ostrog*.[1]

Feeling himself strong enough to defy the Chinese, Tolbusin, in March, 1686, ordered a company of three hundred men to go down to the river to gather tribute. This action touched off the second major war. At the Khumarsk the Russians came in touch with forty Chinese soldiers who had been sent by the Chinese authorities at Tsitsihar to ascertain whether it were really true that the Russians had reestablished themselves at Albazin. When the Chinese learned of the reconstruction of Albazin, the Emperor ordered Sapusu and Lang Tan to make preparations for a new attack. China ordered its army to advance from Aigun assisted by a navy on the Sungari. On July 7, 1686, it arrived before Albazin and surrounded the fort from all sides, allowing neither entrance nor exit by land or water. The fields were laid waste and the crops destroyed and an estimated one thousand Russian soldiers were besieged. In the bitter fight many lives were lost and governor Tolbusin was mortally wounded. His place was filled by Beiton. The siege lasted for more than three months at the end of which time the Russian garrison was reduced to one hundred and fifty men. Provisions and ammunitions had run out, and the Russian soldiers in beleaguered Albazin suffered a great deal from infectious diseases. The Russian situation was desperate, and the Chinese might have exterminated them without great difficulty.[2]

Fortunately for the Albazin garrison, Russian diplomacy intervened at this time to relieve the beseiged Albazin. Early on November 15, 1685, Moscow had received the Emperor's edict to the commander of Albazin, dated 1682, which called upon the Cossacks to avert war by retiring from Albazin. The Csar who was then fully occupied with wars in the Baltic, and who had come to the realization that the Emperor of China was more than a mere tribal chieftain, decided to send an embas-

---

[1] Ravenstein, *op. cit.*, pp. 47–49.
[2] *Ibid.*, pp. 50–52. *P'ing-ting lo-cha fang-lüeh*, in *So-fang pei-ch'eng*, preli. Chüan II, p. 16.

sy of peace to Peking immediately. Two advance agents, Nicephore Venyukoff and Ivan Favoroff were ordered to proceed to the Chinese capital to announce the forthcoming arrival of the Russian plenipotentiary. Due to lack of proper communication, however, Moscow's policy was not made known to the local authorities in Siberia. While the peace mission set out from Moscow, the Russians in Nerchinsk reoccupied Albazin,[1] bringing about the second war, which we have already described, in 1686.

When the war was going on on the Amur, the Dutch ambassadors, Paats and Keyzer arrived in Peking.[2] K'ang-hsi, continuing to cherish hopes of peace, uncertain whether his letters to Moscow had reached their destination and whether the behavior of the Locha actually received the sanction of the Csar, and still ignorant of the imminent arrival of the Russian mission, decided to make the Dutch ambassador the bearer of another dispatch from him to the Csar. On September 4, 1686, two months after the commencement of the second war of Albazin, instructions were given to the court ministers to prepare a letter for the Csar to be sent by the Dutch ambassadors. After reviewing the Amur situation and complaining that the Russians never answered his letters, K'ang-hsi had the following to say:[3]

Learning that our army had withdrawn, the Locha have returned to Yaksa and rebuilt the city. Since we have repeatedly dispatched decrees to them but have not received a single reply and since on the contrary they are defending Yaksa without respite, we wonder whether the difficulty of travel through the Nipchu (Nerchinsk) districts may have prevented our previous dispatches from reaching their destination, and whether the Locha at Yaksa, being criminal fugitives may have found it impossible to return to their home country. Now I have just discussed the matter with the tribal envoy from Holland. He remarks that his country is adjacent to Russia and that their languages are mutually comprehensible. You will prepare a letter containing our ideas expressed in our previous dispatches. Let it bear the seal of the Board of War, and be handed to the Dutch ambassador to be delivered to the Tsar of Russia. It is our desire to recover the districts of Yaksa and Nipchu, and to delimit the territory with a boundary line which must not be trespassed. This will enable the inhabitants of both sides to live in permanent peace and friendship. When the Tsar gives his reply, his dispatch bearer should come directly by land. But if traffic by land should be difficult, he should deliver this reply to the Dutch government which will forward it to us.

This was China's first definite proposal to Russia for the delimitation of the frontier. The government of Russia was differentiated from the

[1] *Ibid.*, preli., Chüan VII, p. 2ab. M. Gaston Cahen, *Histoire des Relations de la Russie avec la Chine sous Pierre le Grand* (1689–1730), (Paris: Librairie Felix Alcan, 1912), pp. 35–36.

[2] Earl H. Pritchard, "The Kotow in the Macartney Embassy to China in 1793," *Far Eastern Quarterly*, II (February, 1943), 202.

[3] *So-fang pei-ch'eng*, preli., Chüan VII, p. 1b–7a, quoted in Chen, *Yenching Journal of Social Studies*, IV (Feb., 1949), 136.

Cossacks on the Amur, who were regarded as irresponsible fugitives fleeing from the Csar's law. With Moscow sending an envoy of peace to China and Peking simultaneously offering to limit its territorial claim on the Amur, the way was paved for bridging the gap between the two empires.[1]

Meanwhile, Venyukoff and Favoroff, the Moscow advance agents, arrived in Peking in September, 1686, with the request on behalf of Csar Peter, who had just ascended the throne in 1686, that the Cossacks violating the Chinese border be punished, the siege of Albazin be raised, and announcing that a special plenipotentiary would be sent to treat the frontier affairs. The letter of the Csar to the Emperor brought by the advance agents, was written in a suitable Chinese style, and runs as following:[2]

With great care and humbleness I heard that your highness is ruling the whole of China with good ministers. The officials are appointed to govern the various parts of the vast land; and subjects comprise Manchus and Chinese. Your renown extends all over the world. Your majesty, the Great Sagacious Emperor, states that my father Alexei Mikhailovich sent Nikolai G. Spathary to your Heavenly court for the purpose of friendship between the two countries. Being ignorant of the Chinese customs and without any civilization, he spoke and behaved barbariously, for which we beg your pardon. As for praising your majesty, there may be something here out of the Chinese style. Please don't condemn it because I am so far away that I don't know anything about Chinese customs and etiquette. Your majesty deigned before to send a letter of which no one in my country knew the meaning. When asked, upon his return, Spathary said that the letter referred to the surrender of the deserter Gantimur and complained of the disturbance of my subjects on the border. Recently I am told that your majesty has sent an army and made attack upon my frontier; it will amount to enmity between the two countries. If my subjects on the frontier offend your border, your majesty may send a messenger to tell me about it and I certainly will punish them severely. It is not necessary to make war upon me. Now I received your decree and know the details. Accordingly I ordered my army not to attack your border when they arrived there. Please ascertain among my subjects who made disturbance and return them to me; I will punish them in accordance with law. Besides sending a plenipotentiary to the border to settle disputes of the border I also dispatched Nicephore Venyukoff and Ivan Favoroff in advance to request that the siege of Albazin be raised. And I still ask that you will write to me. If so, everything will be settled and we will have peace forever.

By this time the Emperor, like the Csar, had his hands full with the problem of Galdan of the Eleuths (Kalmuks) in the northwest. Consequently any settlement by peaceful means of the Amur conflicts which befitted China's position as an empire would be welcomed by Peking. And so upon receiving this letter, the Emperor was pleased by the Csar's

---

[1] Chen, *Yenching Journal of Social Studies*, IV (Feb., 1949), 136–137.
[2] *So-fang pei-ch'eng*, preli., Chüan VII, pp. 6b–7.

humility and immediately ordered Sapusu to raise the siege of Albazin and let the Russians pass freely in or out of the city, but to forbid plunder. The order sent by the Emperor to the front runs:[1]

We had no intention of carrying out a massacre; our desire was to let them off easily. Sapusu and his colleagues are hereby ordered to withdraw their troops from Yaksa (Albazin). He can at the same time notify the Locha inside the town that they are free to pass in and out, but must not commit any depredations. The rest can stand over until the Russian envoys arrive.

At the end of November 1686, this order arrived at the front and the Chinese immediately retired from the neighborhood of the city. It was an unconditioned truce. In May, 1687, the Chinese withdrew still further. During the truce the beleaguered were at liberty to leave the fort to buy provisions and other necessities, and even to admit reinforcements. The Chinese general even supplied the Russians with provisions and offered to send surgeons to look after the sick Russians. On August 30, 1687, the Chinese left Albazin altogether and returned to their former quarters at Tsitsihar and Aigun. The Russians rebuilt their villages and cultivated their fields anew, but they were not permitted to hunt, as the Chinese looked upon this as an infringement of their rights of sovereignty. It is due to the lenient policy of China that peace was secured before the two countries succeeded in negotiation.[2] A full account of the diplomatic transactions which eventually brought about peace will be given in the next chapter.

---

[1] *Ibid.*, p. 7ab.
[2] Ravenstein, *op. cit.*, pp. 52–53.

CHAPTER IX

THE TREATY OF NERCHINSK

I. THE DISPATCH OF EMBASSIES

The increasing complications between China and Russia on the Amur frontier made it appear desirable at Moscow to come to some arrangement regarding the frontiers of the two empires. The chancellor Nicephore Venyukoff, accompanied by Ivan Favoroff, was sent to arrange preliminaries, as has been mentioned above. He left Moscow in December, 1685 and arrived at Peking in September, 1686. At Peking he succeeded in inducing the Emperor to order the Chinese general to lift the siege of Albazin, which, as stated above, actually took place on November 30, 1686. Venyukoff brought back a letter from the Emperor to the Csar. Though addressed to the "great, white Lords, Brethren, Tsars and Autocrats," its contents were first to be communicated to the governor of Siberia. As the letter conveys a good idea of the Chinese manner of thinking with regard to Russian operations on the Amur, we reproduce it here extensively. It may help in understanding the stay of the siege of Albazin and the negotiation of the treaty. It is dated November 12, 1686.

The officers to whom I entrusted the supervision of the sable-hunter have frequently complained of the injury which the people of Siberia (Sokha) do to our hunters on the Amur, and particularly to the Ducheri. My subjects have never provoked yours, nor done them any injury; yet the people at Albazin, armed with cannons, guns, and other firearms, have frequently attacked our people, who had no firearms, and were peaceably hunting. Moreover, they gave shelter to our deserters; and when my Superintendent of the Chase followed some deserters of Kandagan to Albazin, and demanded their surrender, Alexei, Ivan, and others responded that they could not do this, but must first apply to the Changa Khan for instructions. As yet, no answer has been vouchsafed to our inquiries, nor have the deserters been given up.

In the meantime, my officers on the frontier have informed of your Russians having carried off some peaceable hunters as prisoners, for instance, Kelera, Solona, and others.

They also roved about the lower Amur and troubled and injured the small town of Genquen and other places. As soon as I heard of this, I ordered my officers to take up arms, and act as occasions might require. They, accordingly, made prisoners of the Russians who were roving about the Lower Amur; no one was put to death, but all were provided with food. When our people arrived before Albazin and called upon it to surrender, Alexei and others, without deigning a reply, treated us in a hostile manner and fired off muskets and cannons. We therefore took possession of Albazin by force, but even then we did not put anyone to death. We liberated our prisoners, but more than forty Russians of their own free choice, preferred remaining amongst my people. The others we exhorted earnestly to return to their own side of the frontier, where they might hunt at pleasure. My officers, however, had scarcely left, when four-hundred and sixty Russians returned, rebuilt Albazin, killed our hunters, and laid waste their fields, thus compelling my officers to have recourse to arms again.

Albazin consequently was beleaguered a second time; but orders were nevertheless given to spare the prisoners and restore them to their own country. Since then Venyukoff and others have arrived at Peking to announce the approach of an ambassador and to propose a friendly conference to settle the siege of Albazin. On this, a courier was sent at once to Albazin, to put a stop to further hostilities.[1]

After the departure of Venyukoff, Feder Alexvitch Golovin was appointed envoy extraordinary to settle the border disputes with China. The first instructions to him, drafted in the early part of 1686, included both political and commercial aspects. Among the political instructions, the Russian representatives were told to propose the fixation of the boundary line along the whole length of the Amur. In case the proposal was rejected, they should make a small concession by fixing the line along the Amur and its tributary, the Bystra. In case the alternative proposal was also rejected, the line should be fixed further north along the Amur and its bributary, the Dzeya or Zeya. The instructions relating to commerce were particularly important. The ambassador was to collect information concerning river routes into China, i.e., the Ob, the Irtish, and the Selenga, to ask for official regularization of trade between the two countries, both export and import; and he was to persuade the Chinese Emperor to send ambassadors to Moscow and to urge Chinese merchants to sell their silk, silver, velvets, spices, ingots and precious stones, etc., in Russia. The ambassador was further instructed to enter into communication with the Mongol princes who might aid him in his diplomatic task.[2]

Golovin left Moscow on January 20, 1687, accompanied by Ivanzin Vlasof, and the secretary Genion Kornitski. His escort was formed by a regiment of Regular Militia (*Stulzi*) fifteen hundred strong and com-

---

[1] Ravenstein, *op. cit.*, pp. 54–56.

[2] Cahen, *op. cit.*, pp. 9–10, quoted in Hsüan-min Liu, "Russo-Chinese Relations up to the Treaty of Nerchinsk, "*The Chinese Social and Political Review*, XXIII (1939–1940), 412–413.

manded by Colonel Fedor Skripizin. The Colonels Paul Grabof and Anton von Smalenberg were to command two other regiments to be raised in Siberia. A Stolnik, Alexei Sinyavin, and five attachés increased the splendour of the embassy. Ivan Loginof was sent forward to announce to Peking the actual departure of the embassy; and after this the Chinese army before Albazin received orders to retire to Aigun, which it did on August 30, 1687.[1]

On September 30, 1687, Golovin received additional instructions from Moscow which were to be kept secret. He was instructed to cede Albazin in exchange for adequate commercial privileges, to avoid, except in case of absolute necessity, any bloodshed, and if all proposals were rejected, he was to inquire when another Russian mission might be sent.[2] Golovin reached Selenginsk on October 22, 1687. While he was on his journey, important messengers were sent out from Peking to Moscow, but again, owing to communication difficulties, they passed each other on the way. The Chinese Emperor's dispatches to the Russian Csar were carried, one by Père Verbiest, and another by Père Grimaldi, both Jesuit priests in the service of the Bureau of Mathematics in Peking. In his messages, K'ang-hsi made complaints about the behavior of Spathary, demanded the return of Gantimur, and informed the Csar of the raising of the siege of Albazin. However, before the arrival of these letters in Moscow, the Csar had issued the above second intsruction concerning further concessions.[3]

Fearing that its concessions might not produce the desired results, the Russian court, at the end of the year, issued further orders to Golovin. The ambassador was instructed to request the Tsetsen Dampa Khutuktu, the high priest of Mongolia, to lend his good offices as mediator between Russia and China, and, if necessary, to prevail on him to make a journey to Peking in that capacity. Accordingly, Golovin sent a messenger to Urga.[4] The Tushetu Khan, brother of the Khutuktu, who had been asked by the Chinese Emperor to watch the arrival of the Russian embassy, immediately reported the news to Peking.[5]

In May 1688, Loginof arrived in Peking, to announce the coming of Golovin and to propose selenginsk as the place for a conference. The Emperor promptly appointed a mission to go to the conference and

[1] *Ibid.*, p. 413.

[2] *Ibid.*

[3] Chen, *Yenching Journal of Social Studies*, IV (Feb., 1949), 138.

[4] Cahen, *op. cit.*, pp. 36–41, quoted in Chen, *Yenching Journal of Social Studies*, IV (Feb., 1949), 138.

[5] *So-fang pei-ch'eng*, preli., Chüan VII, p. 26.

fixed Selenginsk as the seat of the conference. The Chinese mission consisted of Prince Songotu as plenipotentiary extraordinary, a member of the Grand Secretariat; Tung Kuo-kang, maternal uncle of the Emperor; Arni, president of the Court of Colonial Affairs; Ma Chi, president of the Censorate; Lieutenant-generals Lang Tan and Pantar-shan; Askaniama Ma-la; Chang Peng-ko, an officer of the Board of War; Chien Liang-tse, provincial graduate; and two Jesuit interpreters, Jean Francois Gerbillon (Chang Ch'eng) and Thomas Pereyra (Hsü Jih-sheng). Before their departure, K'ang-hsi requested the envoys to deliberate on the terms on which China should come to agreement with Russia. They submitted a memorial as follows:

> Nipchu was originally the pasture lands of our Maomingan tribe, and Yaksa was the old home of Peilile, our Dahur Chieftain. The territory occupied by the Russians is not theirs, nor is it a neutral zone. The Amur has a strategical importance which must not be overlooked. If the Russians descend it, they can reach the Sungari. If they descend the Sungaria to the south, they can reach the Naun, the Khumara, Kirin and Ninguta, and the land of Sibos, the Khorchins the Solons, and the Dahurs. If they descend the Sungari to the mouth, they can reach the sea. Into the Amur flow the Amgum, the Bystra, and the Dzeya. Along these rivers live our people, the Orochons, the Gilyaks, the Birars, as well as the Hochen, and the Feyak. If we do not recover the entire region, our frontier people will never have peace. Nipchu, Yaksa, and all the rivers and rivulets flowing into the Amur being ours, it is our opinion that none should be abandoned to the Russians. Gantimur and other deserters must be extradited. If the Russians will accede to these points, we shall in return give up their deserters, repatriate the prisoners, draw the boundary and enter into commercial relations; otherwise, we shall return and make no peace with them at all.[1]

The memorial was approved by the Emperor on May 19, 1688, and the mission, provided with a guard of eight thousand troops, left Peking for Selenginsk by way of Mongolia. At this period the Mongols were not yet subject to the sway of China, and the wars between the Khalkas and Eleuths broke out, as we have already related. The war endangered the onward progress of the embassy, so it was ordered to return to Inner Mongolia to prevent the mission from falling into the hands of the Eleuths. Meanwhile a letter was dispatched to Golovin, then at Udinsk, acquainting him with the reason for the non-appearance of the Chinese embassy.

Golovin and his party arrived at Selenginsk from Udinsk sometime in the summer (or fall) of 1688. In Udinsk and Selenginsk the Golovin mission was attacked by the Khalka Mongols in revenge for the previous Russian brutality inflicted upon the Mongol tribes. When the khalkas turned their forces against Galdan who was invading

---

[1] *So-fang pei-ch'eng*, preli., Chüan VII, p. 1ab.

Khalka territory, Golovin succeeded in breaking out of the Khalka siege. In March, 1689, he, attacking with his military force some khalkas in the area of Selenga River, even scored a victory over them and forced them to accept Russian suzerainty.[1] While in Udinsk and Selenginsk, Golovin, in view of the troubles in the area, had sent a gentleman of his suite, accompanied by sixty-three persons, to Peking to request China to choose a safe place nearer the frontier for conference, and to inquire how many persons would accompany the Chinese embassy so that Russia might appear with an equal number. In reply the Chinese chose Nerchinsk as the place of conference and stated that the ambassador should not have his suite exceed the number for his personal safety. Meanwhile, the Chinese messengers returned and brought a letter from Golovin, saying that he earnstly desired to come to a final settlement regarding the frontier affairs, and that he had sent men to Peking through Nerchinsk to arrange the peace conference. The Emperor now called the Songotu embassy back to Peking from Inner Mongolia.[2] From Peking the embassy was to start a new journey to Nerchinsk.

K'ang-hsi understood a diplomatic principle-speak softly and carry a big stick. The Emperor was anxious to settle the frontier disputes with Russia in order to deal with Galdan with full strength. Therefore, before the departure of the mission, K'ang-hsi gave instructions to the envoy to make concessions, if necessary. The instructions read as follows:[3]

> If we retained Nipchu and insisted upon not giving it to the Russians, then their envoys and merchants would find no place for shelter, and their intercourse with us would become difficult. At the beginning of the conference you and the Chinese plenipotentiaries should still endeavor to keep Nipchu, but if their envoys beg for that city, you may draw the boundary along the river Argun.

In comparison with Golovin's second instructions, these revised instructions to the Chinese delegation do not seem to run counter to the Russian demands. The negotiations might, therefore, be expected to succeed.

On June 13, 1689, the Chinese ambassador Songotu and his suite were ordered to leave Peking for Nerchinsk by way of the Amur. He had the same suite as before, but the troop was increased by fifteen hundred men on the Amur. On reaching the Kherlon River (July 16),

[1] Sebes, *op. cit.*, pp. 57–59.
[2] Ravenstein, *op. cit.*, pp. 57–59.
[3] Tsiang, *Tsinghua Journal*, VIII, Pt. 1 (Dec., 1932), 24–25. *Ping-ting lu-cha fang-lüeh*, in *So-fang pei-ch'eng*, preli., Chüan VIII, 1b.

they sent a messenger in advance to inform Vlassof, the governor of Nerchinsk, of their approach. On July 11 they arrived opposite Nerchinsk and the barges, which had preceded them in great number, ranged themselves along the banks of the Shilka in front of the Chinese camp, hoisting their colors in honor of the plenipotentiaries. Then followed numerous armed junks and soldiers. The force was around ten thousand men with seventy-six barges. Besides, they had three thousand to four thousand camels and at least fifteen thousand horses. The governor of Nerchinsk naturally felt uneasy in the presence of so large a force. The Chinese ambassador said that the prior arrival of the boats was contrary to the Emperor's orders, and in order to quiet uneasiness, commanded them to retire a few versts, and all awaited the arrival of Golovin. The governor of Nerchinsk presented the Chinese embassy with ten oxen, and fifteen sheep, the former in the name of his Czar, the latter in his own. The three Russian officers who presented the presents each received a piece of silk in return. Soon a messenger from Golovin arrived who told of the state of the roads as the occasion of the delay.[1]

2. THE NEGOTIATION OF THE TREATY

At last, on August 18, 1689, Golovin and his suite arrived at Nerchinsk. Two days were spent in preliminary arrangements, and the conference commenced on the 22nd. Before the conference began the Russians insisted that it should be held with an equal number of men on each side. The controversy was finally settled by the agreement that the Russians could have an equal number of men to accompany their representatives to the place of meeting. Five hundred should remain at some distance from the place of the conference, and another 260 should attend the envoys on the spot, carrying no arms but swords. To avoid treachery it was agreed that the Chinese should be with the Russians, and the Russians with the Chinese. In order that there might be an equality in everything, the ambassadors were to meet under their tents which should be placed side by side as if the two were one, and they should sit in their tents one over against another without any superiority on either side.[2] Eventually a larger tent was set up for both sides according to the principle of equality. The Russian

---

[1] Ravenstein, *op. cit.*, pp. 58–59.
[2] *Chinese Respository*, VIII, 419, quoted in Weigh, *op. cit.*, p. 11.

portion was neatly fitted up and was set off with Turkish carpets; while the Chinese portion was plain with a long bench in the middle. The two embassies, heavily guarded on both sides with colors flying and kettledrums beating, proceeded to the tent. The Russian alighted first to do the honors of their country and, advancing a few steps to meet the Chinese, invited them to enter the tent first. They sat opposite each other on benches with a table between them. The interpreters sat at the upper end of the table, while the retinue stood. Each side had five hundred soldiers placed close to the fort where the tent was pitched, and forty officers and 260 soldiers followed the envoys. After all had taken seats in the tent, the conference began.[1]

The first conference opened with some questions of etiquette, both sides beginning with exhorbitant demands. Golovin proposed the Amur as the future boundary between the two empires. In return the Chinese demanded surrender of Albazin, Nerchinsk and Selenginsk and proposed the boundary should be on the line of the Lake Baikal and the Stanovoi Mountains.[2] Golovin was not prepared to make so great a concession, and the conference ended in a most unsatisfactory manner. In the second conference, the Chinese offered to permit the Russians to retain Nerchinsk, but simply as a trading post, being aware of the fact that the Russian traders might disturb the border without a trading center. This proposal was scouted like the first by the Russians; the Chinese left in high dudgeon, prepared to strike their tents, and refused to confer with the Russians any further.[3] But Songotu demanded that each side should grant to the other letters declaring what had passed in the two conferences, that the accounts might be rendered to their respective governments. A rupture of negotiations seemed to be in sight.

On the third day the impasse continued, but thanks to the efforts of the Jesuits, an agreement was reached. The Jesuits paid a visit to the Russian camp and declared that the Chinese certainly would not feel satisfied unless Albazin were ceded. The Jesuit's good office is recorded in Pere Gerbillon's diary as follows:[4]

[1] Ravenstein, *op. cit.*, pp. 59–60.

[2] The Stanovoi Mountains are called Outer Khingan Mountains by the Chinese. They are not to be confused with the Great Khingan Mountains which lie south of the Amur, between the Argun and the Naun Rivers.

The Pereyra diary records differently: "At first our ambassadors proposed the town of Nipchu as the border line, leaving the town itself to the Moscovites." in Sebes, p. 237.

[3] Ravenstein, *op. cit.*, p. 60.

[4] P. F. B. Du Halde, Jesuit, *Description of the Empire of China and Chinese-Tartary, Together with the Kingdoms of Korea and Tibet*: containing the geography and history (natural as well as civil) of those countries. (London: Edward Cave, at St. John's Gate, 1741), II, 312

The 25th in the morning.... Soon after the Deputy returned, P. Pereya and I, as tho' of our own heads went privately to wait on the Plenipotentiares, who no less desirous of peace than ourselves, seemed very well pleased at our coming. We first declares to them that if they were not resolved to surrender Yaksa, and the country about it, it would be in vain to give themselves any more trouble because the ambassadors had express orders not to treat without that concession; that as for the country from Yaksa to Nipchu, and to the north of the river Saghalian, we could not precisely tell how far our people would abate of their demands; that they themselves were judges in what place between those two towns they could be satisfied to fix the bounds of the two empires; and that we did not doubt but our ambassadors, out of their desire to peace, would do all in their power to obtain it. The Russian Plenipotentiary answered that since it was so, he desired our ambassadors to let him know their last resolution; on which we returned to report this answer to them. It rained also this day and night.

On August 26, a Russian deputy was sent to the Chinese camp to inquire what their minimum terms were. The Chinese drew a line on the map running along the river Kerbechi or Gorbitsa and through the great chain of the Outer Khingan Mountains which stretched north-eastward to the North Sea, i.e., the Sea of Okhotsk. Thus they proposed that the territories west of the river and north of the mountains should belong to Russia, and the region east of the river and south of the mountains should belong to China. South of the Kerbechi the boundary should follow the river Argun. The Chinese also indicated that the Russians should not advance into the territory of the Khalkhas, who had recently submitted to the Emperor of China.[1]

After the departure of the Russian deputy, the Jesuits went to see the Russian Plenipotentiaries and demanded their terms. On behalf of the Chinese Embassy they also proposed the delimitation of the boundary between Outer Mongolia and Siberia. The Chinese government was anxious to extend protection to its Khalkha subjects. Golovin refused to entertain the last proposal, since its scope was not covered by the Csar's instructions and the Khalkhas as the enemy of Russia should not enter the peace treaty at all. As to the Argun boundary, Golovin raised the question concerning a number of buildings which the Russians had constructed east of that river. When these were reported to the Chinese delegation Songotu readily agreed that the determination of a boundary for Outer Mongolia should be left for the future, and that the Russian buildings east of the Argun should be pulled down and the material transported to the other side of the river to be restored to the Russians.[2]

[1] Chen, *Yenching Journal of Social Studies*, IV (Feb., 1949), 142–143.
[2] Ibid., p. 143. Sebes, *op. cit.*, p. 245.

While an agreement seemed to have been reached, the Russians suddenly reverted to their original stand. They insisted on their retention of Albazin, and proposed that the boundary should run from the source of the Kerbechi, and then, not to the Outer Khingan Mountains, but through the course of the river Amur to its mouth. As soon as the Jesuits heard of this, they reproached the Russians with being insincere and left the conference.[1] On hearing this the Chinese called a council. It was resolved to surround Nerchinsk, to incite the neighborhood natives to revolt, and send men down the Amur to take Albazin. The Russians, on the other side prepared for defense; the fortifications of Nerchinsk were strengthened, and the town was barricaded. An open rupture seemed inevitable.[2]

However, hostilities were not looked forward to with confidence by either party. The Russians would have lost Albazin, while China needed a peace settlement with Russia so as to concentrate its power to suppress the Eleuths' rebellion commanded by Galdan. When, therefore, a Russian interpreter crossed over to the Chinese camp to ask for renewed negotiations, they gladly availed themselves of the opportunity. Gerbillon was again sent to the Russian camp, this time in the fortress of Nerchinsk, to find out the exact terms of the Russian offer. The Russian delegation proposed a draft treaty in which the following articles should be included: first, that in letters which might be written by the Chinese Government in the future to the Csar, the titles of the latter should be inserted either at length or in brief, and that no terms should be used which might express a superiority of the sovereign of either state; secondly, that ambassadors on both sides should be honorably treated, that they should deliver their credential letters into the respective sovereign's own hand, and should be at full liberty in the places where they resided; thirdly, that there should be free commerce between the two empires, and that the subjects of each might, with permission of the governors, be at liberty to go wherever they pleased within their jurisdictions, and trade out of one empire into the other. To the first and second demands, the Chinese delegation answered that as they had no instructions from their Emperor, and since China had never yet sent ambassadors to any other kingdom, they could say nothing, that neither was it their business to regulate the style of their Emperor's letters, but they assured the Russian delegation that the subjects of the Csar, and much more his ambassa-

[1] Chen, *Yenching Journal of Social Studies*, IV (Feb., 1949), 143
[2] Ravenstein, *op. cit.*, pp. 60–61.

dors, would always be treated with respect in China. They also readily agreed to the third article, but refused to insert it in a treaty, saying that a matter of such small consequence was not proper to be joined with the weighty affair of the regulation of the boundary.[1]

This conference marked the first occasion in which a European power demanded of China the acceptance of a definite pattern of international relations. It included the equality of nations, the exchange of diplomatic representatives, and their direct access to the head of the state, and the freedom of commerce between China and Russia. While this pattern of intercourse was generally accepted in the West, it was inconsistant with the traditions of the Chinese Empire, and therefore repugnant to its monarch. China invariably rejected these demands. In matters of trade, Chinese envoys deemed it expedient to meet the Russians half way, and accepted the Russian proposal but refused to insert it in the treaty regulating the boundary. In fact, the major purpose of Golovin's mission was to secure free trade with China, and so the article relating to free trade had to be put into the treaty at length.

The Chinese rejection of the Russian demand for equal treatment was natural. Throughout her history of imperial period China considered herself the civilized center of the world as she proudly called herself Chung Kuo (middle kingdom) or T'ien Hsia (the world under heaven) with her Emperor known as T'ien Tse (son of heaven). She claimed the superiority of her civilization and took an arrogant attitude toward the foreigners. Since in her foreign relations her only experience was to receive tribute bearers from the barbarians, she treated the Western envoys in the same manner after she came contact with Western nations. Kowtows and the presentation of tribute were required of them as evidence of their acceptance of Chinese suzerainty and their respect for Chinese civilization. However, the manner in conducting the negotiation at Nerchinsk, the style of the writing of the treaty and the procedure of signing the treaty show some Chinese concessions to the Russian demand for equality. China was willing to yield her traditional superior attitude for the reason of political necessity. K'ang-hsi Emperor was anxious to have peace with Russia in order to concentrate his effort on defeating Galdan of the Kalmuks. He also wanted a very strict treaty binding the Russians, so that the border troubles would be avoided.

But the main reason for the Chinese concessions was the advices of

---

[1] Du Halde, *op. cit.*, II, 313

the Jesuits to K'ang-hsi Emperor and to the Chinese ambassadors to the peace conference. The Jesuit missionaries in Peking had been introducing Western arts and sciences which proved useful to China. As K'ang-hsi Emperor himself became very much interested in Western knowledge, some jesuits like Pereyra and Gerbillon were actually counsellors, advisers and teachers of the Emperor. They who had acquired the knowledge of the Law of Nations in Europe must have taught it to the Emperor. Moreover, they had been the inter-mediaries in the Sino-Russian diplomatic transactions; it was logical for K'ang-hsi Emperor to have Peryera and Gerbillon included in the Chinese peace delegation. As Peryera reveals in his diary, by sending him and Gerbillon along with the delegation the Emperor also wanted everything done according to the principles of the Law of Nations. To show his confidence in them the Emperor gave Peryera and Gerbillon his own dresses and proclaimed in public: "I am treating you with the honor and distinction that I accord to my grandees whom you shall accompany to negotiate important affairs." Because of the Emperor's personal trust in the two Jesuits, the Chinese ambassadors paid much respect to their advices during the course of the negotiation. They not only play the role of intermediary but also contributed important ideas.[1]

In Peryera's diary, the Law of Nations was mentioned many times. According to the Law of Nations, equality and reciprocity were the bases of negotiation, and he persuaded the Chinese ambassadors to accept the principles and to treat the Russian as civilized equals. Good faith was essential in international transactions, and he complained that both the Russians and Chinese were lacking it. He talked about the concept of just and unjust war to prevent the Chinese from starting a war against the Russians when the negotiation was on the verge of rupture. All these exhortations were taken by the Chinese ambassadors as the fundamentals of the negotiation. Other details such as writing, signing, sealing and exchanging of the treaty also closely followed the practices of the Law of Nations. Even the oathtaking was prescribed according to the Christian fashion.[2] It is the contribution of the Jesuits that for the first time some principles and practices of the Law of Nations were introduced into China when the treaty of Nerchinsk was negotiated and signed.

Concerning the delimitation of the boundary, soon a new difficulty arose. It was realized that the Stanovoi Mountains (the Outer Khingan

---

1 Sebes, *op. cit.*, pp. 107–119.
2 *Ibid.*

Mountains) did not end at the coast but divided into two chains; the major one, called Nosse (the present Stanovoi Mountains) turned northward, while the minor one curved southward, not ending at the coast. Between these two chains lay a vast country watered by the River Udi. Around the river, the choicest sables, black foxes, and other furs were found, and along the shore, huge fish. It was a rich land which both countries desired to possess. The Chinese declared that they had designated the Nosse, while the Russians insisted that they had consented to the minor chain as the boundary. Negotiations were discontinued.[1]

On September 2, 1689, the Chinese envoys, in a somewhat difficult situation, plainly saw that by aiming at more than they had orders to demand, they ran the risk of breaking off the negotiation, concluding nothing, and by so doing, incurring punishment from the Emperor. Pereyra and Gerbillon advised them that the Russian envoys would not consent to the Chinese demands. The Jesuits were again to be sent to the Russian envoys to renew the negotiation by proposing the division of the country in question. On September 2, 1689, just before the Jesuits' departure, the Russian envoys sent a letter to the Chinese envoys, showing their sincerity in concluding a peace treaty by proposing to leave the boundary in the disputed country undecided. With this the Chinese delegation was satisfied.[2]

On September 3, the Jesuits went to the Russian encampment, and secured an agreement that the lands lying between the two chains of mountains should remain undecided till both sides had informed their monarchs and learn their resolutions.[3] By that time the delegates on both sides were perhaps too weary to bring up any further problems. The Gantimur issue was dropt by the Chinese because he died before the negotiation. Realizing that his heirs would not have so much influence upon other tribes as he, the Chinese did not press for their extradition in the negotiation. Instead they merely proposed that in the future no fugitives from one country should be harbored by the other.[4] Basic decisions were thus accomplished and they started to draft the text of the treaty.

The main purpose of K'ang-hsi Emperor's desire for concluding a peace treaty with Russia was to stop Russian aid to Galdan in his war against the Khalkas which had come under Chinese suzerainty. In July,

---

[1] Du Halde, *op. cit.*, p. 314; Sebes, *op. cit.*, p. 265.
[2] *Ibid.*, pp. 265–271; Du Halde, *op. cit.*, p. 314.
[3] *Ibid.*, p. 314; Sebes, *op. cit.*, pp. 271–273.
[4] Chen, *Yenching Journal of Social Studies*, IV (Feb., 1949), 146–147.

1689, Galdan sent Bachoktu Khan to Moscow for improving friendship in the hope that Russia would be his ally against the Khalkas and the Chinese. In March, 1690, when Golovin was on his way back to Irkutsk, Galdan sent a courrier to Golovin to deliver a letter proposing an offensive alliance against the Khalkas and the Chinese. But Golovin refused to discuss the proposal, for he felt that the Treaty of Nerchinsk which had just been concluded prevented such a discussion. Meanwhile, on the basis of the treaty, K'ang-hsi Emperor warned the Russians of the consequences of the proposed alliance between Russia and the Eleuths, as he gave the following imperial decree to a Russian envoy who had just arrived at Peking:[1]

... ... Galdan has made it widely known that in alliance with the troops of your country he is planning to start another attack on the khalkas. Now the khalkas have submitted themselves to the rule of our dynasty. If you mistakenly form an alliance with him, it would be a breach of faith on your part, and you would give cause for another war. You may immediately dispatch two fast riders to the chiefs at Nipchu and tell them that they must publicly announce our warning to the Russian subjects.

If the treaty had not been signed by China and Russia, there was great possibility that Russia would make an alliance with Galdan of the Kalmuk Sungars (or Eleuths) against the Khalkas and the Chinese. If so, it would be very difficult for China to defeat Galdan. But K'ang-hsi Emperor had foresight to forestall the possible alliance between Russia and the Eleuths by concluding the treaty, so that he was to have a free hand to defeat Galdan in 1696. The Emperor's wisdom was evidenced by his remarks before his ministers on the peace with Russia on the Chinese New Year's Day of 1690:[2]

... ... Again, in the pacification of the Russians, both Manchu and Chinese ministers advised me that the matter could hardly succeed since Russia was far away from China. But I said this matter could not be dropped. So immediately I sent higher officials [to Nerchinsk] to proceed with [negotiation with the Russians] according to my instructions. As it turned out, Russia was brought to terms. I have not been bragging of my own success. I am not like you people who will get someone to eulogize your slightest achievement.

3. THE TREATY OF NERCHINSK, 1689

At length the draft of the treaty was agreed upon, and on September 7 the signatures were exchanged in a tent pitched for this purpose.

---

1 Tang-ping chun-ko-êrh shu-lüeh [A Brief Report of the Suppression of the Sungars], in So-fang pei-ch'eng, chüan IV, p. 4a.
2 Shêng-chao [Imperial Decrees], No. 1, in So-fang pei-ch'eng, preliminary chüan I, p. 23a.

The Chinese Plenipotentiaries appeared in state and signed and sealed the Manchu and Latin copies. The Russians came in like manner, and signed and sealed the Russian and Latin copies. The Russians handed one copy in Latin and one in Russian to the Chinese, and the Chinese handed one copy in Latin and one in Manchu to the Russians. The Latin copies were signed and officially sealed by both parties, and therefore were regarded as official.[1] After this, the ambassadors rising all together, and holding each the copies of the treaty, swore in the name of their sovereigns to observe them faithfully, taking Almighty God, the sovereign Lord of all things, to witness the sincerity of their intentions. Jesuit Gerbillon said that K'ang-hsi had given express orders to the Chinese ambassadors to swear the peace by the God of the Christians, because he believed that nothing could influence the Russians more to an inviolable observance of the peace than their knowing it was sworn in the name of the "true" God.[2]

According to the authoritative Latin text, the Treaty of Nerchinsk consisted of six articles: (1) the boundary between the two empires was fixed along the Argun, continuing along the Amur to the mouth of one of its tributaries, the Kerbechi, thence northward along the Kerbechi up to its source, to the Stanovoi Mountains, and thence eastward along the crests of the mountains to the source of the Udi River. The Valley of the Udi lying between the northern and southern branches of the Stanovoi Mountains remained neutral territory. All the Russian houses and dwelling which were then situated to the south of the river Argun were to be removed to the north bank of the river; (2) Albazin was to be destroyed, and the garrison was to be withdrawn; (3) everything which had occurred before the stipulation of the treaty was to be buried in eternal oblivion, but the deserters from one country to the other in the future would be liable to extradition; (4) subjects of either party who were in the domains of the other at the conclusion of the treaty were allowed to remain where they were; (5) only those subjects who were provided with passports were allowed to "come and go" for the purpose of trade; (6) the terms of this treaty were to be observed in strictness and carried out without infraction. In a supplement to the treaty, it was stipulated that boundary stones were to be erected on the frontier, and that on these stones were to be engraved

---

[1] See Appendix I: The Text of the Treaty of Nerchinsk. Compare the official Latin text and Pereyra's Latin text in Sebes *op. cit.*, pp. 157–160; Pereyra's Portugese and English diary in Sebes, *op. cit.*, pp. 282–287.

[2] See Appendix II: The form of the oath of the Chinese ambassadors.

the terms of the treaty in the Manchu, Chinese, Russian, and Latin languages.[1]

In 1690, Emperor K'ang-hsi, in accordance with the provision of the supplement, ordered boundary stones to be placed on the Kerbechi, and other frontier spots. On the stones were engraved the terms of the treaty. The inscriptions, however, did not contain the full text, but gave merely a summary of the articles. Besides the four languages mentioned, a fifth, Mongol, was added. Chinese official records most unfortunately neglected the text in its original complete form, and kept only the summary as inscribed on the boundary stones. Among other omissions, it does not include the stipulation concerning the neutralization of the Udi basin.[2] Such a summary form was later adopted by the *T'ung Shang Yo Chang Lei Tsuan*[3] in 1886, and Customs' treaties[4] in 1908 and 1917, and caused many a discrepancy in the explanation of the treaty.

The summary form of the treaty is not the only source of discrepancies. The different texts of the treaty gave rise to discrepancies also, especially in respect to the neutralization of the Udi basin. There are three versions regarding the eastern border line of the Udi basin. The first version is that provided by the Latin text, according to which the portion of territory between the northeastern branch of the Stanovoi Mountains and the Udi River were to be left undemarcated for the time being, since the two plenipotentaries were unfamiliar with the geography of the region. It was to be demarcated after an investigation by the two countries. The second version is that provided by the Manchu texts, according to which the portion between the Udi River and the southeastern branch of the Stanovoi Mountains was to remain undecided. The third version is that provided by the Russian texts according to which, in addition to the statement made in the Manchu texts, the Udi River belongs to Russia, and the southeastern branch of the Stanovoi Mountains to China.

In spite of the fact that Latin was considered by both sides to be the accepted common language, and the Latin version was signed, sealed,

[1] See Appendix I. *Chin-tin huang-chao wen-hsieng tung-kao*, in *So-fang pei-ch'eng*, preli. Chüan XI, p. 13ab.

[2] Chen, *Yenching Journal of Social Studies*, IV (Feb., 1949), 148.

[3] Li Hung-chang, et al., *T'ung shan yo chang lei tsuan* [China's Treaties of Commerce, an Analytical Classification], (Tientsin: Governmental Printing Office, 1886), XXIII, 1ab; XXIV, 1a; V, 286.

[4] *The Chinese Maritime Customs, Treaties, Conventions, etc., Between China and Foreign States*, 2nd ed., (Shanghai: Statistical Department of the Inspectorate General of Customs, 1917), I, 3–7.

and exchanged as authoritative, we must make inquiry into the historical facts as to which version is more acceptable in reference to the real intentions. According to Pereyra's and Gerbillon's diaries, the Chinese plenipotentiary first made a draft of the treaty in Manchu. Regarding the disputed Udi basin between the northern and the southern branches of the Stanovoi Mountains, the Chinese revised the article in Manchu according to the compromised decision of neutral land on September 2 and sent the text to the Russians. The Russian plenipotentiary was satisfied with it. On September 4, the Russians drafted the treaty in Russian, the Jesuits and the Russian interpreters made a Latin translation and sent it back to the Chinese. The Chinese found that the Russian draft concerning the Udi basin was contradictory to the compromise reached before. The Russian plenipotentiary was informed of this discrepancy, and agreed to have that particular article revised when the authoritative text in Latin was drafted. On September 6, the Russians sent their interpreters to the Chinese side, with the help of the Jesuits, to draft the Latin text according to the sense of the Chinese plenipotentiary. On September 7, Gerbillon, together with the Russian plenipotentiary, and his interpreters drafted the Latin duplicates of the treaty.[1] Since the intention of the two parties had been made known, the Latin version should be considered authentic.

Although the Latin text provided that the territory of the Udi River was to be left undemarcated until the case had been reported, the boundary of that portion was never demarcated thereafter. During the conference at Kiakhta in 1727, the Chinese plenipotentiary proposed a demarcation of that territory, but the Russians rejected the proposal. According to Article VII of the Treaty of Kiakhta, the boundary line of that region was still left undrawn. Whether the Russians refused to demarcate this region because of the provision in the Russian text which gave the territory along the Udi River to Russia, or because of other intentions, we do not know. However, when the treaty of Aigun was signed in 1858, the region was finally incorporated into the Russian dominion.[2]

4. THE CONFIRMATION OF THE TREATY

In 1692, Csar Peter the Great dispatched Evert Isbrant Ides, a German in his service, on a mission to the Chinese Emperor with the

---

[1] Du Halde, *op. cit.*, II, 314.
[2] Liu, *The Chinese Social and Political Science Review*, XXIII (1939–1940), 440.

purpose of confirming the treaty of 1689, and of improving the commercial conditions of the two countries. He set out from Moscow in March, 1692, and spent 18 months in traveling. He took the same route Spathary had followed, and on arrival at Tsitsihar (the Nuan River in Spathary's journey) was honorably met by Chinese officials. After compliments were passed, both the Chinese and Russians rode forward together till they reached the town where a very good house was provided for Ides, while those of his retinue were well lodged according to their status. On November 3, 1693, he reached Peking. After three days of repose, Ides was given a reception dinner. He was surprised by the abundance of the Chinese dinner, describing the dinner in his memoirs as follows:[1]

After which table was covered with odd meats as roast geese, chickens, pork and mutton, besides all sorts of fruit and confection; the table appointed for me alone was about an ell square upon which the dishes that were all of silver, and piled one upon another, amounted as I told them, to the number of seventy.

On November 12, the Emperor gave Ides an audience in which He presented his credentials. He approached the court, and performed the ceremony in the same manner as Spathary; the kotow and prostrations were by no means dispensed with.[2] After an exchange of compliments, the Emperor dismissed the ambassador to the embassy court.

However, the Emperor read the Csarial letter and was dissatisfied with the form because the Csar's name stood before that of the Emperor. He ordered the letter as well as the tribute presented by Ides to be returned, and only because Russia was situated at a distance, and because the Csar knew nothing about the Chinese system, did he order that the letter should be corrected and the ambassador should be made acquainted with the right style. Also by grace the ambassador was permitted to sell the merchandise he had brought. It was ordered, however, that thereafter Russian letter to the Emperor should be opened by the Chinese Governor on the Amur and examined to see whether the style was appropriate or not. If it was inappropriate, the Governor should turn the letter back on the border. Only after the Governor deemed the style appropriate, could the envoys be admitted to come to Peking. And upon arrival at Peking, the envoys should put the letter and tribute on a table covered with yellow cloth outside the

---

[1] E. Y. Ides, *The Three Years' Land Travels of His Excellency E. Y. Ides from Moscow to China.* (London: Freeman, 1706), p. 68.

[2] Weigh, *op. cit.*, p. 18.

entrance to the imperial palace at the Wu Gate (Wu Men), and then perform the ceremony of kotowing i.e., three prostrations and nine knockings of the head on the ground (*san-kuei chiu-kou*). The ambassador was forced to accept this imperial order.[1] Evidently China was uncompromising on the traditional ceremony, but in view of the threat of Galdan, she in general treated Ides' mission honorably to maintain the friendship with Russia.

To return to the confirmation of the treaty, in 1691, the Moscow Government received the report that a band of Siberian Mongols had deserted their Russian overlords and had gone over to their Mongol brothers across the Chinese frontier. Meanwhile, though Russian caravans had arrived in Peking several times, they were in a state of uncertainty. Russia was not satisfied with such conditions. To regularize Russia's commercial relations with China, and to settle the problem of the deserters, the Csar gave to Ides instructions which may be divided into two parts. The first part concerning commerce, included first, an invitation to Chinese merchants to visit Russia with ingots of gold and silver, precious stones, spices, figured stuffs, and other Chinese products. Secondly, Ides was to take advantage of every opportunity in Peking to study market conditions such as resources, products, prices, customary charges, and to ascertain the Russian products suitable for import into China, and the Chinese commodities most useful to Russia.

The other part was concerned with diplomatic matters. Ides was to conform to Chinese custom, to send gifts and presents to the Emperor and to find out the latter's attitude toward the Treaty of Nerchinsk, and the unsettled frontier problems. He was also to press Russia's claims to the allegiance of the Siberian deserters and to demand their extradition. Lastly he was to ask for a site in Peking for a Russian Orthodox Church which would be built at the expense of the Csar.[2] Here it should be pointed out that the major intent of the instructions was: to establish good commercial relations, to settle frontier problems, to claim the allegiance of the Siberian deserters and to demand their extradition, and to find out the Chinese attitude toward the Treaty of Nerchinsk. These are closely related to the Treaty of Nerchinsk; and some of them were directed toward carrying out the treaty. In regard

[1] To Tsin et al., *Hui tien shih li* A Collection of Statutes of the Ch'ing Dynasty, 1818, Chüan DCCLXIV, Li-fan yuan, p. 3a.
[2] Cahen, *op. cit.*, pp. 80–84, quoted in Chen, *Yenching Journal of Social Studies*, IV (February, 1949), 53.

to this, Weigh, in his *Russo-Chinese Diplomacy*,[1] and Dudgeon in his "Russian Ecclesiastical Mission" [2] explained that Ides mission was dispatched for the purpose of exchanging ratifications. Since Ides did not have express orders to exchange ratifications and, furthermore, since we cannot find in either the Chinese or the Russian sources any record of the exchanging, one can hardly say this mission was intended for this purpose.

However, the purpose of the mission was to secure some commercial privileges and to settle some diplomatic problems in accordance with the Treaty of Nerchinsk. In other words, Ides tried to make some detailed arrangement with the Chinese Government to fulfill what the treaty had provided. Events connected with the Ides mission prove the sincerity of both sides in carrying out the treaty. In 1693 while the Ides mission was still in Peking, Russia sent back two Chinese deserters from Siberia; to this, the Chinese sent a letter of acknowledgment. Some Russians crossed the definite border southward to hunt; China wrote to the *voevoda* at Nerchinsk, asking him to call them back and to punish them, and not to let them cross the border in the future. China also warned that if the *voevodas* were unable to restrict their subjects, China would have to ask the Csar to punish them, since they did not observe the provisions of the Treaty of Nerchinsk. Consequently in 1695, Russia sent back to China the deserter Han-to who, as a minor leader of the Tsetsen Mongols, had rebelled against China and fled to the Russian side.[3] Concerning trade Ides' mission obtained a special arrangement from the Chinese Government which will be fully explored in the next chapter.

We may then conclude that by deeds the Treaty of Nerchinsk was confirmed. Through Ides' mission both the Chinese and the Russian Governments knew each other's attitudes toward the Treaty of Nerchinsk. The significance of Ides' mission in respect to the confirmation of the Treaty was, in effect, tantamount to that of an exchange of ratifications. After concluding his mission, Ides left Peking in February, 1694, and reached Moscow in January of the following year.

In the Treaty of Nerchinsk, China concentrated on the demarcation of the boundary, while Russia emphasized the establishment of commercial relations. According to the Treaty, not only the present Manchuria belonged to China, but also the land south of the Stanovoi

1 Weigh, *op. cit.*, p. 18.
2 J. Dudgeon, M. D., "Russian Ecclesiastical Mission," Pt. 3, *The Chinese Recorder and Missionary Journal*, III–IV (1870–1872), 339.
3 To Tsin, *op. cit.*, p. 46.

Mountains, north of the Amur and east of the Ussuri to the Pacific coast, including Sakhalin Island. For China the demarcation of such natural boundaries as the Stanovoi Mountains on the north and the Pacific coast with many ports on the east was advantageous for national defense and convenient for communication and transportation. The reason why China could attain such favorable results are twofold: (1) Russia did not have strong forces in the Far East, lacked the geographical knowledge of the Far East, and felt it unnecessary to exploit the Far East on a large scale; (2) China treated the matter wisely; making vigorous military preparations on the one hand and granted some concessions to Russia in the negotiations. As a result, China retained a vast land.

The Treaty also gave China a free hand to defeat Galdan and his Eleuth tribe, when they made war on the Khalkhas and China, as we have mentioned. In 1690, China, in accordance with the purpose of the Treaty to maintain peace between the two empires, warned Russia not to give help to Galdan. Consequently in 1696, Russia refused to lend help when Galdan sought it. With regard to the Russian purpose of establishing commercial relations, Russia, by the Treaty and the supplementary arrangements made by the Ides' mission, secured the establishment upon a firm footing of her trade with China and the right of her merchants to enter China for purpose of trade.

CHAPTER X

THE ECONOMIC AND CULTURAL RELATIONS [1]

I. THE TRADE BETWEEN RUSSIA AND CHINA

As has been mentioned, one of the primary motives which led Russia to conclude the Treaty of Nerchinsk was the prospect of commercial relations with China. It was the commercial motive that led Russia to expand toward the East, and it was this motive which caused her to send so many diplomatic missions to China. Europe was then in the age of mercantilism, and the Russian Government sought to promote its China trade in line with the mercantilist doctrine. By means of a code of definite, stringent regulations Moscow set up a systematic, absolute control over the China trade. Only imperial merchants, i.e., those armed with official sanction, could participate in the trade. The route to be taken, and the commodities imported and exported, were subject to government regulations. Most missions dispatched by Russia to China, in addition to seeking free trade with China, were actually charged with trade, and therefore in many cases, we have found that the Russian Government provided the missions with government treasure for the purpose of trade. Such transactions as would bring into Russia ingots of gold and silver were especially encouraged. Custom dues were levied and collected in the form of bullion so as to obtain precious metals for the government treasury.[2]

Moscow attached great importance to trade with China. As early as 1608 a trading embassy was dispatched by *voevoda* Vasili Vasilievich Volinski of Tomsk to the "Golden Khan" (Altin Khan), with whose help it was hoped to reach China. The mission was a government caravan in the charge of accredited envoys. With the caravan went three Cossacks, an interpreter representing the *voevoda*, and two

---

[1] Cultural relations refer to Russian missionaries in China.
[2] Cahen, *op. cit.*, chap. ii.

Kirgiz princellings who undertook to act as guides and convoy the party to China through the territories of the Altin Khan to whom they promised to present the Csar's envoys. The caravan was interrupted by the civil strifes among the Mongolian tribes and never even reached the Altin Khan. It was Russia's first attempt to trade with China, but it proved abortive.[1]

In 1638, the Khalka, Tushetu and Tsentsen Khans presented Russian guns to the Manchus. Evidently the Mongols had established commercial relations with Russians long before that time. After Mongolia was secured to China, the Chinese government appointed officials to manage Russian trade at Urga (Kulen) and Kiakhta. Hence Urga and Kiakhta became famous as Russian trade centers.[2]

Russian diplomatic missions were often commercial missions as well. In 1655 Baikoff was treated as a merchant by the Chinese. Baikoff denied that he was a merchant, but as a matter of fact, he was charged with two missions: diplomatic and commercial. His commercial mission can be proved by his report to the Csar.[3]

Such goods as were brought to the compound from the shops, were bought at a great price compared to the Russians; and those camels and horses which were sold for silver, into that silver lead and copper had been melted – not one-half was silver; also they brought silver vessels for sale, and those too, all of them, had copper mixed. Pearls were dear, twice as dear as our Russian pearls; as to precious stones, we saw none of any value, nor was there any demand for Russian merchandise, save only for ermine and pesti (Arctic foxes, white or blue "Vuples lagopus"); there were sables and foxes and beavers and leopards in plenty, but it was impossible to buy.

In 1660, the Perfilieff and Ablin mission had the same double objectives as Baikoff's. They were supplied a sum of five hundred Roubles by the Russian treasury with instructions for what to buy in China; and for what Chinese goods the Russian goods might be bartered.[4]

In 1670, Milovanoff was sent to China by the *voevoda* of Nerchinsk without provision from the government treasury. He had nothing to trade. However, he searched for commercial information by visiting shops and inquiring of merchants and made a detailed report to the Russian government. The Chinese, in turn, asked him about the prices

---

[1] Baddeley, *op. cit.*, p. 34.

[2] *Chin-tin ta-ching Hui-tien* [Royal Collection of Statutes of the Ch'ing Dynasty] in *So-fang pei-ch'eng*, preli. Chuan XII, p. 1.

[3] Baddeley, *op. cit.*, p. 147.

[4] *Ibid.*, p. 169.

of Russian commodities. There is no doubt that Milovanoff, in addition to his political mission, had commercial interests.[1]

The mission of Spathary in 1676 gives fuller evidence that the diplomatic mission was also a commercial mission. To prove this true, some quotations may be taken from his report to the Csar, as follows:

July 10th, The Askaniama came alone, and asked if the merchandise belonging to the Treasury and to the Ambassador himself was selling off. The Ambassador answered that there was no sale for the government goods, and business generally was very slack; only the Cossacks had sold a little, of necessity, as best they could.

The reason business languishes is that the interpreter has made a bargain with the mandarins' people; and they beat and drive away, in our presence, the (genuine) merchants, not allowing them to buy anything from us. For the interpreters want to buy everything themselves, and at the lowest prices; it is the same with purchasing, no sellers are allowed in and if this goes on, no freedom whether to buy or to sell, what sort of friendship and love can there be between the two great empires?[2]

The buying and selling went on badly; silks and satins and velvets were sold (by the Chinese) in one shop only, because the mandarins and all the interpreters and merchants have agreed together what prices they would give for our goods, and what they would take for their own – so as to get all the profit; and no one dared to raise the price they offered, or lower what they asked us; so they bought from us just as they pleased, and sold to us at far higher prices than formerly. However, what Russian goods they bought and at what prices, will be set down separately.[3]

These are parts of the description of the commercial tansactions of the Spathary's mission. The transactions may be divided into two kinds: government and individual. Spathary was charged with the state busines. Besides he also had his own personal business, and other members of the mission also carried on trading activities.

As the Russians moved into the Amur, local trade developed between them and the natives. When the Amur conflict began to shape up Askaniama Ma-la was ordered by the Emperor to go to the Solons to prepare military supplies. On returning, he reported to the Emperor that the Russians in Yaksa were living on rice grown around the city, and that those at Nerchinsk had traded with the Ba-erh-hu of the Tsetsen Khan, and that to defeat the Russians it was necessary to destroy the rice fields and prohibit the Mongols from trading with the Russians. In 1682 the Emperor gave a strict order to the Tsetsen Khan that all the tribes under the Khan's control should not trade

[1] *Ibid.*, pp. 201–202.
[2] *Ibid.*, p. 379.
[3] *Ibid.*, p. 396.

with the Russians. This was the first time that China prohibited trade with the Russians.[1]

In 1689 the sixth article of the Treaty of Nerchinsk provided that persons should be permitted to carry on commerce and to sell or purchase at pleasure, provided they were furnished with passports. Regular trade between China and Russia was for the first time stipulated in the treaty. After that, Russia and China often reciprocally traded indigenous goods on the border.[2]

Following the Treaty of Nerchinsk, it was more evident than before that the Russian government sent to Peking men who bore the title of diplomatic agents but whose mission was primarily commercial. Late in 1689, after the conclusion of the Treaty of Nerchinsk, Golovin sent an agent ostensibly to inform the Chinese government that the treaty stipulation concerning the removal of the Russians on the southern banks of the Argun could not be carried out until the following spring. The agent, accompanied by a suite of eighty to ninety persons, arrived in Peking in May, 1690. The Emperor remarked that "in all appearance this company of them came only to trade, and had brought 60 wagons loaded with skins." Similarly in August, 1691, the Emperor made another remark that "a Russian envoy arrived on the frontier of Tartary subject to this Empire, with a retinue of 40 persons, and that about 90 merchants came along with him to trade according to custom." Again in 1692, the Russian agent Atanasius Sopronoff arrived at Peking with a caravan of seventy-two men.[3] According to Chinese records the Csar dispatched envoys to pay tribute to China after the conclusion of the Nerchinsk Treaty.[4] These envoys were received by the Chinese court.

However, the Treaty of Nerchinsk merely stipulated that "the subjects of either nation, being provided with proper passports, may come and go across the frontier on private business and may buy and sell." Nothing was mentioned of caravans, much less of their regular admission into the imperial city – Peking. Because Russia's commercial aspirations were only slightly realized in the treaty, Russia still endeavored to trade with China under the guise of political missions. Strange to say, the Emperor, contrary to established custom in China,

---

[1] *O-lo-ssu wu-shih shih-mu*, [Account of Trade Between Russia and China], in *So-lang pei-ch'eng*, Chüan XXXII, p. 3ab.

[2] *Ibid.*, pp. 9b–13a.

[3] Du Halde, *op. cit.* II, 327–344, quoted in Chen, "Chinese Frontier Diplomacy: Kaikhta Boundary Treaties and Agreements," *Yenching Journal of Social Studies*, IV (Feb., 1949), 151–152.

[4] *Chin-tin Hwang-chiao Wen-hsien tung-Kao*, in *So-fang pei-ch'eng*, preli. Chüan XI, p. 139.

not only raised no objection to the arrival of the Russian caravans, but even went so far as to order them to be housed, entertained, and even supplied with necessities at the expense of the Chinese government, although it was specified that the favor was not to be regarded as a precedent. The reason why China extended special favors to these Russian merchants was that China intended to win the Csar's neutrality in the war against Galdan of the Eleuths.[1]

The Russian caravan trade in Peking was not provided for in the treaty, and hence the continuance of the trade was uncertain. The Ides mission aimed to legalize the situation, and it was agreed that a Russian House (O-lo-ssu Kuan) [2] was to be set up to lodge all Russians who would come to Peking for trade or other purpose. Russian traders could come to Peking every three years for the purpose of trading goods; each time the total number could not exceed two hundred persons. They must have camels and afford transportation at their own expense. All goods would be free of duty, but they were forbidden to trade in commodities prohibited in China. They could live in the Russian House, but China would not supply food and pay other expenses. They could only remain for a period of eighty days; after that period they should return to Russia.[3] This was the official agreement of trade between Russia and China. The trade on the Amur border provided in the Treaty of Nerchinsk was now extended to Peking as a consequence of the conclusion of this agreement. Though China granted only a restricted system of caravan trade, the agreement met in part the desire of Russia.

Ides was allowed to sell all the merchandise which he brought to China in his caravan of some four hundred men when he set out from Moscow. On returning, he was able to draw up a list of commodities suitable for export to China and a list for importation into Russia. Since the task intrusted him had been primarily commercial in nature, it may be said that Ides' mission was not without important results.

China's stipulation that Russian caravans should visit Peking only once every three years and that each caravan should consist of not more than two hundred men was at first not strictly kept. Between 1698 and 1718 – a period of twenty years – ten caravans were admitted into the imperial city. The first of these caravans was that of Lyangus-seff and Savatyeeff, consisting of nearly three hundred secretaries,

---

[1] Du Halde, *op. cit.*, II, 330–344.

[2] The Russian House was set up beside the bridge of the Chungyu River in Peking.

[3] *O-lo-ssu wu-shih shih-mu*, in *So-fang pei-ch'eng* Chüan XXXVII, p. 4a.

servants, and other employees. The movements of the caravan were duly communicated to the *voevodas* of Irkutsk and Nerchinsk.[1] Moscow also sent dispatches to the Khutuktu at Urga and to Songotu in Peking, informing them of the coming of the caravan, and requesting that it be granted passage through Manchuria, that it receive the necessary supply of horses and provisions, that it be protected on its journey within China's territorial domains and that it enjoy the liberty of free trade in Peking.[2] On their return from China the merchants gave a report to the *voevoda* of Nerchinsk. It gave the prices of furs and of Chinese merchandise in Peking, stated that Chinese silver was of base quality while its gold was rare and costly, and that Russia could not expect to obtain much bullion from the China trade. The Chinese on their part complained of the superabundance of Russian goods and of the over-frequency of the caravans. However, no difficulties were placed by the Chinese government in the way of the Russian trade.[3]

In the beginning the Russians came to China for trade via Manchuria. Later they traversed Mongolia into China. Gregory Anthanasius Oskolkoff, head of a caravan which visited Peking in 1700, made a report that a journey from Nerchinsk to Peking via Manchuria took one hundred and fifty days, while a route from Selenginsk through Mongolia, by way of Urga and Kalgan, only required seventy days.[4] The Manchurian route had been designated for the caravan trade by the Russian government, because the Mongolian route was barred by the Galdan war. Now when the Galdan war was over and peace had been restored in Outer Mongolia, the Russian caravans could travel by the Mongolia route. Oskolkoff's report pointed out the advantages of the Mongolia route. Impressed by this report, later caravans traveled by this route. Therefore the Kiakhta, Urga, Kalgan and Peking line was the most important trade route between Russia and China in later centuries.

Generally speaking, the preliminary trade between Russia and China was carried out by diplomatic missions. After Russia had expanded into east Siberia, Russians and Chinese exchanged goods on the border of Mongolia and Manchuria. The Treaty of Nerchinsk of 1689 first regulated the trade on the border. After 1693 the practice of Russian trade in Peking was officially established. In the next century the trade

---

[1] Cahen, *op. cit.*, pp. 96–98, quoted in Chen, *Yenching Journal of Social Studies*, IV (Feb., 1949), 156.

[2] *Documents in Russian*, No. 4, quoted in *Ibid.*

[3] Cahen, *op. cit.*, p. 98, quoted in *Ibid.*

[4] Cahen, *op. cit.*, pp. 99–100, quoted in *Ibid.*, p. 157.

became prosperous on the Mongolian border, and Kiakhta was opened as a trading center in the Treaty of Kiakhta of 1727.

2. RUSSIAN MISSIONARIES IN CHINA

The Greek Orthodox faith had long since become the religion of Russia. Following the eastward expansion, Orthodox missions were dispatched to Siberia in order to convert the aborigines. The missionary work in Albazin was regarded as the start of propagating the Russian religion in China. In 1655, at Albazin a church consecrated to "Savior of the World" was built. After Russians rebuilt Albazin in 1661, Moscow decided to garrison the fort with a strong regiment. In 1672 a governorship was decreed for Albazin and Russian priests began their work of converting the natives to Christianity. The Peking government reacted promptly, and frequent Sino-Russian conflicts occurred on the Amur. Many Chinese prisoners and deserters were taken by the Russians, and many Russian prisoners and deserters by the Chinese. Many Chinese prisoners were baptized in the church at Albazin and were subsequently sent to Yakutsk, while most of the Russians were taken to Peking to form a Russian company under the "Yellow Banner" being settled in the northwestern corner of Peking. Some of the Russians gave up the Christian faith, but others still remained Christians. In 1676 Spathary recorded that, in the absence of an orthodox church, these Christian Russians frequented the Roman Catholic Church. This record promoted a momentous development. In 1685 a group of Russians leaving Albazin for Peking, took with them icons, church vessels, and above all, a Russian priest.[1]

The priest was Father Maxim Leontyev who was mistakenly called Drinitry or Vasily by many others. Unwilling to go, he was taken by force, his wife and son accompanying him. After the Russians settled in Peking, a Greek Orthodox Church, named for St. Nicholas the Miracle-Worker, was established in a former Buddhist temple. Father Maxim was its pastor. For the convenience of his work, he rapidly accommodated himself to the customs around him, shaving his head in the Manchu manner, for example. Yet he did not fail to fulfill his duty. He converted to Christianity the Chinese wives of the settled Russians and the women's relatives.[2]

[1] Albert Parry, *Russian Missionaries in China, 1689-1917* (Chicago: University of Chicago Libraries, 1938), pp. 8–9.

[2] *Ibid.*, p. 10. The Chinese wives were given to the Russians by the Chinese Emperor.

As a result, he was presently encouraged by his superior in Siberia. In 1695 the Metropolitan Ignatius of Tobolsk sent to Peking a priest and a deacon as assistants to Father Maxim. They carried with them church books and vessels and a communion cloth, for those brought a decade earlier from Albazin were now insufficient in consequence of the increasing number of the faithful. To Father Maxim they also brought the Metropolitan's blessing, together with the expression of his satisfaction in regard to Maxim's successful conversion in China. The Metropolitan also instructed the Peking priest to continue the good work of converting the Chinese and even to seek the conversion of the Chinese Emperor, K'ang-hsi.[1]

The idea of converting Chinese to Greek Orthodox was not novel. In 1676, Spathary the envoy had written:[2]

> Now the Jesuits think that soon all the Chinese will be Catholic .... we, however, believe that with God's help and the Tsar's happy fortune, the Chinese will ere long adopt the Orthodox Greek faith.

In 1697, Leibnitz, the great German philosopher, wrote of his hope that the Csar would spread "not merchantilism, but piety and virtue from Moscow to China." Unlike Spathary, Leibnitz foresaw the Russian missionary work in China not as competing with that of the Jesuits or of any other Christians, but as proceeding in perfect harmony with other such efforts. He exercised influence upon the Csar Peter. And it was probably through him that Peter decided to influence China with the Orthodox faith.[3]

In 1693 Isbrant Ides led a mission to China and asked for a site in Peking for a Russian Orthodox church to be built at the expense of the Csar.[4] It was agreed upon that a priest should be sent to minister to the religious wants of the Russians in Peking. It was agreed that the church would not be built until the conclusion of Kiakhta Treaty in 1727.[5]

In 1698, Csar Peter heard from Vinius, an official in Toblosk, that in Peking a Russian church, i.e., Saint Nicholas Church, had been built and a number of Chinese converted to the Greek faith. The Csar was favorable to the work and the next year he wrote to Vinius to continue the work with due propriety:[6]

---

[1] Parry, *op. cit.*, pp. 10–11.
[2] Baddeley, *op. cit.*, p. 430.
[3] Parry, *op. cit.*, p. 14.
[4] Chen, *Yenching Journal of Social Studies*, IV (Feb. 1949), 153.
[5] Ravenstein, *op. cit.*, p. 13.
[6] Parry, *op. cit.*, p. 13.

It is a fine thing, only for God's sake act in this matter cautiously and with no hurry, so as not to anger either the Chinese or the Jesuits who for a long time have had there a nest of their own. For this reason we need there priests not so much learned as sensible and tactful, in order to avoid arrogance which may bring the holy work to a most grievous downfall, as once happened in Japan.

Peter did not have a high degree of respect for the church, but he always used it for the good of the state. Hence it was logical for him to support the work of the Orthodox missionaries in China. His prudence was due to shrewd diplomatic considerations as well as motives of political expediency.

Therefore in 1699, as a result of an agreement made by Ides in 1693, Csar Peter sent a priest by the name of Archpresbyter Vasily Alexandrov to China. He was attached to the caravan conducted by Lyangusseff and Savatyeeff, and ostensibly served the caravan merchants. He held many services for the Russian church, to which the Russian merchants were allowed to come under the armed escort of three or four Chinese. Because the Chinese authorities considered one priest, Father Maxim, to be sufficient, Father Vasily returned to Siberia with the merchants.

Actually the church and the services therein were not strictly observed according to the Orthodox point of view. Lyangusseff and Savatyeeff brought to governor Nikoliev at Nerchinsk a sad tale of what they had seen in the Russian Church at Peking.[1]

The liturgy is sung by the priest Maxim, and he says that it is impossible for him to do it properly on account of his great age and failing eyesight, and there are no deacons there with him, only his son has learnt to read and helps him in the service; and the church warden is Dmitri Grigoroff who is not married and he bakes the wafers, but is illiterate.

Such a condition, of course, needed to be improved, but the Metropolitan of Tobolsk and Father Maxim were powerless to improve it. Not long afterward, the task of the Siberian Metropolitan was taken over by the civil authorities of Tobolsk and Moscow, in fact by the Csar himself. In 1700 Csar Peter issued a special ukase ordering the establishment of a permanent Greek Orthodox Mission in the Chinese capital, for the purpose of converting to Greek Orthodoxy the Chinese Emperor and his people. The Russian church, using the Russians in Peking and their half-blind priest as an opening wedge, "entered China first in the closest alliance with and indeed as an organ of the Russian government." [2]

[1] *Ibid.*, p. 11. Baddeley, *op. cit.*, II, 430.
[2] Parry, *op. cit.*, pp. 11–12.

CHAPTER XI

SUMMARY AND CONCLUSION

Within the area of northern Asia, certain geographical characteristics influence historical developments. Due to the low slope of the Ural Mountains, access to the Russian plain is free. In Asia, though an uninterrupted chain of mountains, deserts, and inland seas constitute certain limits, there are several gateways to the southern part of Asia. The plain itself is divided into two distinct zones: the forest zone in the north and the steppe zone in the south. As the steppe zone is contiguous to the gateways into the plain, it lures nomadic invaders, whereas the forest zone serves as a place of hiding and refuge for people fleeing from these invasions.

On the plain, history can be traced back many centuries before our era. In the third century B.C. tribes of Indo-Iranian stock invaded the Russian steppe zone from Asia. This was the first time that Asiatic tribes invaded Russia. These tribes were followed by numerous others, all migrating from Asia to Russia and each one forcing the other to move westward into Europe. The decaying Roman Empire particularly offered an opportunity for expansion of the Asiatic tribes.

At that time and for a few centuries to come, Russia was a great vacuum, open to the invasion of nomadic tribes. Following the Indo-Iranian tribes, came the Turko-Mongol tribes. They expanded into Russia up to the forest zone, from the Urals to Scandinavia and the White Sea where the Finnish people dwelt. They were warlike and restless, and thus sufficiently dynamic to play a role in history. The vast area north of China and east of Persia, which may be considered their home, was in the first centuries of our era in a state of flux for several reasons: In the second century B.C. China, already a great empire under the Han dynasty, was concerned with Central Asian trade. The necessity of protecting the trade routes led China to wage war against the Turko-Mongol tribes. The Chinese set the Turko-Mongol tribes in motion. The immediate victim of that motion was Russia.

A kind of human whirlwind began which gradually reached Russia. At first the nomads, pressed by the Chinese, started moving westward. Persia also exerted pressure on them and the Turko-Mongol tribes were forced to march beyond the Caspian Sea where they invaded Russia. The great Hun invasion swept over Russia and under Attila, pressed as far as Western Europe.

In the fifth century the Hsiung-nü Empire arose. The Chinese had considered these tribes as a kind of dependency and the emergence of such a power was naturally a serious menace to China, hence a constant effort was made by China to subdue the Hsiung-nü.

In the seventh century, the Arabs conquered central Asia and spread the Moslem faith by force. The nomad tribes could not settle down but had to keep following those who had started their westward drive, and so new invasions continued to splash over the Russian plain.

After the Avars and the Khazars lost their nomadic character, the savage and bloodthirsty nomads, the Pechenegues and the Black Bulgars, came into Russia in the ninth century. But in their turn they had to give place to the Polovtsy or Cumans in the eleventh century. In the thirteenth century when Jenghiz Khan built up the Mongol empire, Russia was again conquered by Asiatic people, but it was merely a final climax to this long list of invasions. Some contacts existed between Russia and China during the two centuries of Mongol domination. Thereafter, thanks to Russian nationalism, Russia threw off the Mongol yoke in 1480. After that, Russia, reversing the usual course of affairs in which the Asiatic people moved into Russia, steadily expanded eastward. She accomplished the occupation of Siberia in the seventeenth century.

By the conquest of Kazan in 1552 and Astrakhan in 1556, Russia at once reached the Ural Mountains and the Caspian Sea. The way into the heart of Asia was now open. In 1587 an expedition under the command of Yermak crossed the Urals and reached the basin of the Ob. In 1587 Tobolsk was built for defense against the native Mongols. By 1620 the Yenisei was reached and the city of Yeniseisk grew up as a center of the fur trade, attracting the natives for barter. In 1632 the fortified port of Yakutsk was founded. From Yakutsk the Russians set about exploring the Amur region. In 1641 the first Russian expedition came to the Amur. In 1645 the Kolyma and the Arctic Ocean were reached. In 1647 an *ostrog* was established at Okhotsk. After the Buriats were defeated, Lake Baikal was reached and Irkutsk was founded in 1651. In 1656 Nerchinsk was established. The Russians built Albazin in 1651 and rebuilt it in 1665. They also built Selenginsk in 1666. At the close of 1682, the Russians had settlements at Albazin on the Dzeya and the Argun. Finally in 1697, a party headed by Atlasor made a long journey on foot and with reindeer from Yakutsk to Anadyrsk, and discovered Kamchatka. At the same time further explorations proceeded across the Bering Straits into Alaska. The Russian conquest of Siberia in the seventeenth century made Russia and China close neighbors, and conflicts occurred on the Amur.

As far back as 1616, a Cossack *ataman* appeared on a self-styled mission from the Csar to the court of the Altin Khan. At this encampment the Russian met the envoy of the Chinese Emperor and secured from the Altin Khan the promise to arrange for a Russian mission to go through to China. The Petlin and Mundoff mission of 1618–1619 is regarded as the first Russian mission actually to reach Peking. In 1654 a Russian ambassador, Baikoff, was sent to China but he refused to submit to "kotow" or the bow of servile allegiance to the Chinese Emperor which was considered a part of the court etiquette for the admittance of any foreign ambassador. Baikoff was thus unpleasantly dismissed by the Chinese court. The subsequent embassies of Perfilieff and Ablin in 1660, of Milovanoff in 1670 and of Spathary in 1676 failed for the same reason. The requirement of "kotow" stems from the Chinese concept of universal empire: China was called the "Middle Kingdom" or "Tien Hsia (the world under heaven)," all foreigners were barbarians, and the only possible attitude towards them was the acceptance of their tribute and submission. The "barbarians of the north," i.e., the Russians, were but another distant tribe whose duty it was, without exception, to send tribute to China. The Russians took the same attitude toward the Chinese. China was no more than a tribe like those in Siberia which Russia had met and subjugated. The Csar tried to summon the Chinese Emperors to accept Russian suzerainty. The Russian ambassadors to China should by no means undergo such a humiliation as kotowing, which the Chinese demanded of them. Ignorant of the political situations and cultural traditions of each other's country, both Russia and China may be held accountable for the failure of these missions.

The purpose of these missions was to make inquiry into the conditions within China, social, cultural, political and economic; to establish diplomatic intercourse and above all to establish commercial relations. China was known to produce gold, precious metal, silk, etc. The

Russians looked upon China as a great future market. Being motivated by the mercantilist theory then prevailing in the West and being depleted of treasure in consequence of wars, Russia was anxious to have a closer understanding with China in order to promote commercial relations. However, Russia followed a very cautious policy toward China. Many a mission was restrained from making direct contact with China in the beginning.

China, on the other hand, felt self-sufficient and had no desire for commerce with the Russians. She adopted a "closed door policy of self-contentment" toward Russia. Besides the Chinese looked down upon merchants and depreciated the importance of commerce. Being used to receiving only tribute bearers the Chinese court lacked the Western concept of trade. Thus the Russian demand for trade could not be easily understood by the Chinese. Both Russian and Chinese policies, added to the difference of the court custom and ceremonial and the ignorance of political conditions of either country, caused the retardation of Russo-Chinese mutual understanding for many years. Nevertheless, China was keenly interested in the security of her frontiers and would not tolerate the encroachment on her tribute tribes made by the new "barbarians" of the north. With her frontier security at stake on the Amur, China was eager to make a settlement with Russia. Milovanoff's and Spathary's missions dealt with some political matters relating to the conflicts on the Amur, but they failed to reach agreement with China.

Although Russia had direct contact with China for several decades the decisive clash between the two empires actually took place in Manchuria. On the Amur the Russians claimed sovereignty over the natives and collected tribute from them. Since the natives had long been subjects of China, then ruled by the Manchus, of course they could not tolerate the Russian expansion. After the Russians had established Nerchinsk and Albazin, they frequented the lower Amur and exacted tribute from the natives there. Such expeditions were essentially the undertaking of private individuals. These Cossack groups were interested in immediate advantage and neglected the future development in the whole area. They killed and plundered the natives; they exacted tribute from the natives beyond what the latter could afford. The Cossacks' actions were enough to bring to the natives' minds pictures of torture, abduction and cannibalism. All the tribes on the Amur hated the Cossacks and did not hesitate to remain in allegiance to China. They requested China to protect them from the

Russian trespassers, and China was thus compelled to decide to expell the Russians. In 1685 a Chinese army advanced upon Albazin. After a blockade of a brief period, the Russians evacuated the fort and retired to Nerchinsk. The Chinese, having destroyed the fort, withdrew to Aigun. The Russians returned almost in the wake of the Chinese and rebuilt Albazin. In 1686, China again made an expedition against Albazin. It was a brief struggle but a sanguinary one. The Russians were surrounded in their fort. At length the seige was raised in consequence of the expected conclusion of a treaty of peace.

Conditions existing in Russia and China inclined both countries to seek peace. Russia was preoccupied with wars in the Baltic. Csar Peter, being a boy just crowned, had not yet consolidated his power. Such circumstances forced Russia to make peace with China. China, on the other hand, was busy in conquering Galdan of the Sungarian Kalmuks, and thus needed peace with Russia and the promise that Russia would not support the Kalmuks. Because both parties did not want war on a large scale on the Amur, the negotiation of a treaty of peace became possible. The negotiation took place at Nerchinsk under the display of force by both sides. After several conferences and aided by the intercession of the Jesuits who introduced some concepts of international law into China for the first time, the treaty was eventually signed in 1689. The important features are: (1) the demarcation of a boundary north of the Amur; (2) the establishment of the practice of extradition; and (3) the establishment of commercial relations. This was the first treaty that China had made with a Western power. It served to maintain peaceful relations between the two empires for more than one hundred and sixty years.

Ides' mission came to China, accompanied by a caravan trade, to confirm the treaty and improve commercial conditions. It was not novel that Russian diplomatic missions dealt with commercial transactions. The establishment of commercial relations was the primary purpose of the diplomatic missions, and most of the previous diplomatic missions of Russia had merchant companies with them. Such a trade was public enterprise, conducted and regulated by the Russian government. However Ides' mission set up a practice of Russian trade in Peking which was to be followed for some time. Therefore Ides' mission may be regarded as an epilogue of Sino-Russian relations in the seventeenth century and also as a prologue to the intercourse between the two empires in the future. Another striking development was the

Russian missionary work in China, which the Russian government utilized as a political instrument. As a result of the Treaty of Nerchinsk and some practices set up in connection with it, China and Russia were able thereafter to carry on peaceful intercourse.

APPENDIXES

I. THE TREATY OF NERCHINSK

(Signed 27th August 1689.)

NOTE–MAYERS, in his "Treaties," p. 96, says of this Treaty: "It was translated from Latin into French by Père Gerbillon, who, with the Portuguese Jesuit, THOMAS PEREYRA, was commissioned by the Emperor K'ANG HSI to accompany the Chinese Plenipotentiaries on their visit to the frontier with the Russian Envoys, and to act as interpreter to the two contracting parties. The Treaty, which was the result of long negotiations, was drawn up in Latin by GERBILLON and his colleague, and translated by the former into French. (See 'Archives diplomatiques,' Paris, 1861, t.i, p. 270, where the French text of the Treaty is given in full.) See also RAVENSTEIN, 'The Russians on the Amur,' p. 62." The French text which follows is from DU HALDE's "Description de la Chine," edition of the Hague, 1736, t. iv, p. 242, but the orthography has been slightly modernised; the English text is a translation from the Russian, made by a member of the Chinese Customs Service; and the Chinese text is from a new (1886) Chinese work entitled *Tung shan yo chang lei tsuan* (China's Treaties of Commerce, an Analytical Classification).

Their Majesties the Grand Dukes Joann Alexeevitch and Peter Alexeevitch, by the Grace of God, Joint Emperors, Czars, and Autocrats of all the Russias, Great, Small, and White; Emperors and Lords over, and successors from immediate and remote ancestors to the Crowns of, many Kingdoms and Countries, Eastern, Western, and Northern; having appointed as their Envoys and Plenipotentiaries Theodorus Alexeevitch Colovin, Minister of the Presence, and Governor-General of Briansk; Ivan Astaffjevitch Vlasoff, Minister of the Household and Governor-General of Elatomsk; and Semën Kornitsky, Deacon of the Orthodox Church;

And His Majesty the Bogdokhan (i.e., Heavenly-appointed Ruler) of China, Supreme Ruler of Great Asiatic Countries, the Most Powerful Monarch, Wisest Ruler, Exponent of Heaven's Law, Most Enlightened Noble, entrusted by Heaven with the government of China for the welfare and glory of its people, having appointed as his Envoys Sag-mu-tu, Commander of the Imperial Body Guard, Grand Secretary, and Councillor of State; Tum-ke-kam, Grand Secretary, Prince of the First Rank, Commander of Banner Corps, and Member of the Imperial Clan; and Lam-tan, Commander of Banner Corps, etc.:

And the aforesaid Envoys having met near Nerchinsk, they have agreed upon the following Articles:

Article I.

The river Gorbitza which joins the Schilka from its left side near the river Tchernaya, is to form the boundary between the two Empires. The boundary from the source of that river to the sea will run along the top of the mountain chain [in which the river rises]. The jurisdiction of the two Empires will be divided in such a way that [the valleys of] all the rivers or streams flowing from the southern slope of these mountains to join the Amur shall belong to the Empire of China [lit. of Han], while [the valleys of] all the rivers flowing down from the other (or northern) side of these mountains shall be similarly under the rule of His Majesty the Czar of the Russian Empire. As to [the valleys of] the other rivers which lie between the Russian river Oud i.e.-Cada and the aforesaid mountains – running near the Amur and extending to the sea, – which are now under Chinese rule, the question of the jurisdiction over them is to remain open. On this point the [Russian] Ambassadors are [at present] without explicit instructions from the Czar. Hereafter, when the Ambassadors on both sides shall have returned [? to their respective countries], the Czar and the Emperor of China [Han] will decide the question on terms of amity, either by sending Plenipotentiaries or by written correspondence.

Article II

Similarly, the river Argun, which flows into the Amur, will form the frontier along its whole length. All territory on the left bank is to be under the rule of the Emperor of China [Khan of Han]; all on the right bank will be included in the Empire of the Czar. All habitations on the south side will be transferred to the other.

Article III

The fortified town of Albazin, built by His Majesty the Czar, is to be completely demolished, and the people residing there, with all military and other stores and equipment, are to be moved into Russian territory. Those moved can take all their property with them, and they are not to be allowed to suffer loss [by detention of any of it].

Article IV

Fugitives [lit. runaways] from either side who may have settled in the other's country previous to the date of this Treaty may remain. No claims for their rendition will be made on either side. But those who may take refuge in either country after the date of this Treaty of Amity are to be sent without delay to the frontier and at once handed over to the chief local officials.

Article V

It is to be understood by both Governments that from the time when this Treaty of Amity is made, the subjects of either nation, being provided with proper passports, may come and go [across the frontier] on their private business and may carry on commerce [lit. buy and sell].

Article VI

All the differences [lit. quarrels] which may have occurred between the subjects [of each nation] on the frontier up to the date of this Treaty will be forgotten and [claims arising out of them will] not be entertained. But if hereafter any of the subjects [lit. traders or craftsmen] of either nationality pass the frontier [as if] for private and legitimate business, and [while in the foreign territory] commit crimes of violence to property and life, they are at once to be arrested and sent to the frontier of their own country and handed over to the chief local authority [military], who will inflict on them the death penalty as a punishment of their crimes. Crimes and excesses committed by private people on the frontier must not be made the cause of war and bloodshed by either side. When cases of this kind arise, they are to be reported by [the officers of] the side on which they occur to the Sovereigns of both Powers, for settlement by diplomatic negotiation in an amicable manner.

If the Emperor of China desires to engrave [on stone] the Articles of the above Treaty agreed upon by the Envoys for the determination of the frontier, and to place the same [at certain positions] on the frontier as a record, he is at liberty to do so. Whether this is to be done or not is left entirely to the discretion of His Majesty the Emperor of China.[1]

II. THE FORM OF OATH TAKEN BY THE CHINESE AMBASSADOR AT MERCHINSK

The War which has been carr'd on by the Inhabitants of the Frontier of the two Empires of China and Russia, and the Battles fought between them with great Effusion of Blood, disturbing the Peace and Quiet of the People, being intirely contrary to the Divine Will of Heaven, which is a Friend to the Publick Tranquillity; We, Ambassadors extraordinary of the two Empires, having been sent to settle the Bounds of both Dominions, and establish a solid and perpetual Peace between both Nations, which we have happily executed in the Conferences held by us in the 7th Moon of the 28th Year of Kang hi, and near the Town of Nipchü, by distinctly setting down in Writing the Names of the Countries and Places where the two Empires join each other have, by fixing the Bounds of both, and ordering in what manner such disputes, as may fall out for the future, are to be treated of; have mutually received an authentick Writing, in which is contained the Treaty of Peace, and have agreed that the said Treaty, with all its Articles, shall be engraven on Stone, to be fixed in the Places appointed by us for the Bounds of both Empires, to the end that all who pass by those Places may be fully informed thereof, and that this Peace, with all its Conditions, may be for ever inviolably observed. But should any one have the Thought only, or secret Design, to transgress these Articles of Peace, or, breaking his Word and Faith, should violate them out of private Interest, or from the Design of exciting new Troubles, and rekindling the Fire of War, we pray the Supreme LORD of all Things, who knows the Bottom of Men's Hearts, not to suffer such People to live out their Days, but to punish them by an untimely Death.[2]

[1] *Treaties between China and Foreign States*, pp. 1–7.
[2] Du Halde, *op. cit.*, pp. 315–316.

BIBLIOGRAPHY

BOOKS

Baddeley, John P. (ed.). *Russia, Mongolia, China*. London: Macmillan and Co., 1919, also 1964.

Cahen, Gaston. *Histoire des Relations de la Russie Avec la Chine sous Pierre le Grand*. Paris: F. Alcan, 1912.

Chang, Mu. *Meng-ku yu-mu chi* [Account of the Nomadizing of the Mongols]. Shanghai: The Commercial Press, 1937.

Chien, Mu. *Kou-shih ta-kang* [Outline of the Chinese History]. Shanghai: Commercial Press, 1937.

Chin-tin huang-chao tung-tien. [Royal General Account of the Ch'ing Dynasty]. Preliminary Chüan X of the *So-fang pei-ch'eng*.

Chin-tin huang-chao wen hsien tung-kao. [Royal Collection of Important Documents of the Ch'ing Dynasty]. Preliminary Chüan XI of the *So-fang pei-ch'eng*.

Chin-tin ta-ch'ing hui-tien. [Royal Collection of Statutes of the Ch'ing Dynasty]. Preliminary Chüan XII of the *So-fang pei-ch'eng*.

Ch'ing shih kao. [Draft History of the Ch'ing Dynasty]. Compiled by the Ch'ing shih kuan. Edited by Chao Erh-hsun et al. Peking: Ch'ing shih kuan, 1927. Also Hong Kong: Wen-hsüeh Yen-chiu shê, 1960.

Ch'ing shih lu. See Ta Ch'ing li-chiao shih-lu.

Cote, W. *Account of the Russian Discoveries between Asia and America*. To which were added the Conquest of Siberia, and the History of the Transactions and Commerce between Russia and China. London: Printed by J. Nichols for T. Cadell, in the Strand, 1780.

Czaplicka, M. A. *Aboriginal Siberia*. Oxford: At the Clarendon Press, 1914.

Davidson-Houston, J. V. *Russia and China* [From the Huns to Mao Tse-tung]. London: Robert Hale Limited, 1960.

Du Halde, P. F. B. Jesuit. *Description of the Empire of China and Chinese-Tartary, Together With the Kingdoms of Korea and Tibet*: Containing the geography and history (natural as well as civil) of those countries. London: Edward Cave, at St. John's Gate, 1741.

Fisher, R. H. *The Russian Fur Trade, 1550–1700*. Berkeley and Los Angeles: University of California Press, 1943.

Golder, F. A. *Russian Expansion on the Pacific, 1641–1850*. Cleveland: Arthur H. Clark Co., 1914.

Howorth, H. H. *History of the Mongols*. London: Longmans, Green, and Co., 1876.

Hsueh, Chang-san & Ouyang, Yi. *A Sino-Western Calender for Two Thousand Years*. Changsha, China: The Commercial Press, Limited, 1940.

Hummel, Arthur W. (ed.). *Eminent Chinese of the Ch'ing Period.* Washington: U.S. Government Printing Office, 1943–44.

Ides, E. Ysbrants. *Three Years' Travel from Moscow to China.* London: Freeman, 1706.

Kerner, Robert Joseph. *The Russian Adventure.* Berkeley & Los Angeles: The University of California Press, 1943.

— *The Urge to Sea.* Berkeley and Los Angeles: The University of California Press, 1942.

Lantzeff, George V. *Siberia in the Seventeenth Century.* Berkeley & Los Angeles: The University of California Press, 1943.

Liu, Ta-pei. *Wu-shih shih-chi chung-kuo li-nien piao* [A Table of the Chinese Calender of Fifty Centuries]. Shanghai: The Commercial Press, 1933.

Liu, Tse-jung & Wang, Chih-hsiang, (ed. and trans.). *Documents in Russian Preserved in the National Palace Museum of Peking, Kanghsi-Chienlung Period.* Peiping National Museum, 1936.

Lobanov-Rostovsky, A. *Russia and Asia.* New York: The Macmillan Co., 1933.

Michael, Franz. *The Origin of Manchu Rule in China.* Baltimore: The John Hopkins Press, 1942.

Ming shih [The History of the Ming Dynasty]. Bk. 9 of the *Erh shih wu shih* [Histories of the Twenty-five Dynasties]. Shanghai: Kaming Book Co., 1934.

Ming shih lu. [Annals of the Ming Dynasty], Edited by Yao Kuang-hsiao et al. 1940.

O-lo-ssu shüeh-kao. [Account of Russian Studies]. Chüan XIII of the *So-fang pei-ch'eng.*

O-lo-ssu wu-shih shih-mu [Account of Trade between Russia and China]. Chüan XXXVII of the *So-fang pei-ch'eng.*

Pares, B. *A History of Russia.* New York: Alfred A. Knopf, 1944.

Parry, A. *Russian Missionaries in China, 1689–1917.* Chicago: The University of Chicago Libraries, 1938. (unpublished).

Pavlovsky, M. N. *Chinese Russian Relations.* New York: Philosophical Library, 1949.

Ping-ting lo-cha fang-lüeh. [Plans of the Suppression of the Locha], Preliminary Chüan V of the *So-fang pei-ch'eng.*

Rand McNally World Atlas. Chicago: Rand McNally & Co., 1950.

Ravenstein, E. G. *Russians on the Amur.* London: Trubner and Co., Paternoster Row, 1861.

Schwartz, Harry. *Tsars, Mandarins, and Commissars* (A History of Chinese-Russian Relations). Philadelphia and New York: J. B. LippinCott Co., 1964.

Sebes, Joseph, S.J., *The Jesuits and the Sino-Russian Treaty of Nerchinsk (1689)* The Diary of Thomas Pereira, S.J. Rome: Institum Historicum S. I., 1961.

Shih-i-chao Tung hua lu. [Annals and Memoirs of the Eleven Emperors of Ch'ing Dynasty]. Edited by Wang Hsien-chien, 1884.

So-fang pei-ch'eng. A collection of various Chinese materials concerning historical and geographical descriptions of northern Asia from very early times up to 1858. Compiled and edited by Ho Chiu-tao. No data of publication is given, but the work was finished and presented to the Hsien-feng Emperor in 1858.

Ta Ch'ing li-chao shih lu. (or Ch'ing shih lu). [Annals of the Ch'ing Dyansty]. No data of publication is given.

Ti, sun. *Shih-chieh ta-shih nien-piao.* [A Calender Table of Leading Events of the World]. Chunking: The Independence Press, 1945.

To, Tsin et al., *Hui-tien shih-li.* [A Collection of Statutes of the Ch'ing Dynasty]. Lifan Yuan, 1818.

Treaties, Conventions, etc. between China and Foreign States. Compiled by

Statistics Department of the Customs, Shanghai. 2nd ed. Shanghai: Customs, 1917.
Vernadsky, G. *Political and Diplomatic History of Russia*. Boston: Little Brown and Co., 1936.
Weigh, Ken Shen. *Russo-Chinese Diplomacy*. Shanghai: The Commercial Press, 1928.
Williams, W. W. *The Middle Kingdom*. New York: Charles Scribner's Sons, 1901.
Yuan shih. The History of the Yuan Dynasty, Bk. 8 of the *Erh shih wu shih*. Histories of the Twenty-five Dynasties. Shanghai: Kaming Book Co., 1934.

ARTICLES

Cahen, Gaston. "Les Relations de la Russie avec la Chine et les Peuplades Limtrophes al fin du XVII Siecle et Dans le Premier Quart du XVIII." *Revue Historique*, XXXII (Mai-Aout, 1907) 45–63.
Chen, Agnes Fang-Chih. "Chinese Frontier Diplomacy: (1) The Coming of the Russian and the Treaty of Nerchinsk; (2) Kiakhta Boundary Treaties and Agreements." *The Yenching Journal of Social Studies*, IV (February, 1949), 99–205.
Chen, Fu-kuang. "Sino-Russian Diplomatic Relations since 1689," *The Chinese Social and Political Science Review*, X (1926), 120–144, 476–508, 711–727, 933–938.
Dudgeon, John. "Historical Sketch of the Ecclesiastical, Political and Commercial Relations of Russia with China," *The Chinese Recorder and Missionary Journal*, III–IV (1870–1872), 143–146; 273–280; 337–425; IV, 10–17.
Galt, Howard S. "The Kuo Tzu Chien – Its Historical Development and Present Condition," *The Chinese Social and Political Science Review*, XXIII (1939–1940), 441–462.
Liu, Hsüan-min. "Russo-Chinese Relations up to the Treaty of Nerchinsk," *The Chinese Social and Political Science weview*, XXIII (1939–1940), 393–440.
Pritchard, Earl H. "The Kotow in the Macartney Embassy to China in 1793," *Far Eastern Quarterly*, II (February, 1943), 202.
Tsiang, Ting-fu. "Tsui-chin san-pai-nien tung-pei wai-huan shih," (A History of Foreign Invasions into Manchuria in the Recent Three-Hundred Years], Pt. 1, *Tsinghua Journal*, Peiping, VIII (December, 1932), 6–52.

CHINESE GLOSSARY

Abahai　阿巴海

Aigun　愛琿

Alexei Mikhailovich　阿列克席米汗羅烏池

Amban Janggin　昂邦章京

Amgum (Hungkung)　恆滾

Ao-chi-erh-tu Khan　鄂濟爾圖汗

Ao-erh-k'um River　鄂爾昆河

Argun River　額爾古納河

Arni　阿爾尼

Baatur (Batir)　巴圖爾

Bahai　巴海

Ba-erh-hu 巴爾呼

Birar 畢喇爾

Buriat 布利亞

Buyandara 巴延達拉

Bystra 牛滿

Chahar 察哈爾

Chang Ch'eng 張誠

Chang Chien 張騫

Chang Mu 張穆

Chang Peng-ko 張鵬翮

Chao Erh-hsün 趙爾巽

Chao-mo-to 昭莫多

Chao-tai ts'ung-shu 昭代叢書

Chasaktu Khan 札薩克圖汗

Che-ling-tse 車棱札

Chen, Agnes Fang-chih 陳芳芝

Chen Fu-kuang 陳復光

Che-pu-tseng-tan-pa-hu-tu-k'e-tu 哲卜尊丹巴呼圖克圖

Chien-hsi tsin-she 漸西村舍

Chien Liang-tse 錢良擇

Chien Mu 錢穆

Chi-lin wai-chi 吉林外記

Ch'ing Dynasty 清朝

Ch'ing shih kao 清史稿

Ch'ing shih lu 清實錄

Chin-tin huang-chao tung-tien 欽定皇朝通典

Chin-tin huang-chao wen-hsien tung-kao 欽定皇朝文獻通考

Chin-tin ta-ch'ing hui-tien 欽定大清會典

Chüan 卷

Chung kuo 中國

Chungyu River 中玉河

Erh-shih-wu shih 二十五史

Erintshin 額琳沁

Fedor Alexvitch Golovin 費要多羅

Feyak 費雅喀

Fukien 福建

Fu-kuo gun 護國公

Galdan 噶爾丹

Galt, Howard S. 高厚德

Galtu 噶爾圖

Gantimur 根忒木爾

Gilyak 奇勒兒

Gorbitza (Kerbechi) River 格爾必齊河

Great Khingan Mountains 大興安嶺

Hai-se 海色

Hami 哈密

Han-to 罕篤

Heilungkiang 黑龍江

Hochen 赫真

Ho Chiu-tao 何秋濤

Hsien-feng 咸豐

Hsi-feng Pass 喜峯口

Hsiung-nu 匈奴

Hsüan-hua 宣化

Hsü Jih-sheng 徐日昇

Huang Peng-nien 黃彭年

Hui-tien shih-li 會典事例

Hungkung (Amgum) 恆滾

Ivan 宜番

Ivan Favoroff 宜番法俄羅瓦

Jehol 熱河

K'ang-hsi 康熙

Kerbechi River 格爾必齊河

Khalka 喀爾喀

Khumarsk 呼瑪爾

Khungdaidgi (Khungtaidji) 琿台吉

Khurkha 庫爾哈

Kiakhta 赤塔

Kirin 吉林

Kuo-shih ta-kang 國史大綱

Kortsin (Khorchin) 科爾沁

Kuang-tsung 光宗

Kuei-hua 歸化

K'u-erh-han 庫爾瀚

Ku-fa-tan tsun 古法壇村

Kulen (Urga) 庫倫

Lan Tan 郎坦

Lang Tan lieh-chüan 郎坦列傳

Liaoning 遼甯

Li-fan Yuan 理藩院

Liu Hsüan-min 劉選明

Li Hung-chang 李鴻章

Liu Ta-pei 劉大白

Liu Tse-jung 劉澤榮

Lobdzang 羅卜藏

Locha 羅剎

Ma chi 馬齊

Ma La 馬喇

Mantsi 蠻子

Maomingan 茂明安

Meng-ku yu-mu chi　蒙古遊牧記

Ming-an-ta-li　明安達里

Ming Dynasty　明朝

Ming Shih　明史

Ming shih lu　明實錄

Nan Hua-jen　南懷仁

Nikolai Gavrilovich Spathary　尼果賴罕伯里爾鄂維策

Nicephore Venyukoff　米起勿兒魏牛高

Ninguta　甯古塔

Nipchu　尼布楚

Norbu　諾爾布

Nü-chi　女真

Nurhaci　努爾哈赤

O-lo-ssu Kuan　俄羅斯館

O-lo-ssu shüeh-kao　俄羅斯學考

O-lo-ssu wu-shih shih-mu 俄羅斯互市始末

Orochon 俄羅春

Oud (Udi) 烏得河

Outer Khingan Mountains 外興安嶺

Pan Ch'ao 班超

Pantarshan 班達爾善

Pasheli 巴什里

Peilile 倍勒兜

P'eng Ch'ung 彭春

Piao 表

Ping-ting lo-cha fang-lüeh 平定羅剎方略

San-fan 三藩

San-kuei chiu-kou 三跪九叩

Sapusu 薩布素

Sarguda 沙瑚達

Sa Ying-nge 薩英額

Shang-chien-wu-he 尚堅為黑

Shang-shu 尚書

Shih-chien ta-shih nien-piao 世界大事年表

Sheng-chao 聖詔

Shih 石

Shih-lang 侍郎

Shih-i-chao tung-hua lu 十一朝東華錄

Shilka (Schilka) 什勒喀河

Shukul Daitshing 書庫爾岱青

Shun-chih 順治

Sibo 錫伯

Sining 西寗

So-fang pei-ch'eng 朔方備乘

Solon 索倫

Songotu 索額圖

Ta-ch'ing li-chao shih-lu 大清歷朝實錄

Tai-tsu 太祖

Tai-tsung 太宗

Tang-ping chun-ko-erh shu-lüeh 蕩平準噶爾述略

Tarbagatai 塔爾巴哈台 (塔城)

Tchernaya 綽爾納河

T'ien Hsia 天下

T'ien Shan 天山

T'ien Tse 天子

Ti Sun 迭生

To Tsin 托津

Tsagan-Araptan 策妄阿拉布坦

Tsetsen Khan 車臣汗

Tsiang Ting-fu 蔣廷黻

Tsinghai 青海

Tsinghua Journal 清華學報

Tsitsihar 齊齊哈爾

Tsui-chin san-pei-nien tung-pei wai-huan shih 最近三百年東北外患史

Tsu-kuang-ko 紫光閣

Tu Li-shen 圖理琛

Tumendara Daitshing 圖們達岱青

T'ung-chou 通州

Tunghai 東海

Tung Kuo-kang 佟國綱

T'ung-shang yo-chang lei-tsuan 通商約章類纂

Turfan 土魯蕃

Tushetu Khan 土謝圖汗

Udi 烏第河

Ujala 烏札村

Uliassutai 烏里雅蘇台

Ussuri 烏蘇里河

Van-li (Wan-li) 萬歷

Wang Chih-hsiang 王之相

Wang Hsien-chien 王先謙

Warkha 瓦爾喀

Wei Yuan 魏源

Wen-hsüeh yen-chiu shê 文學研究社

Wen-tsung 文宗

Wochi 窩集

Wu Men 午門

Yaksa 雅克薩

Yakutsk 雅庫

Yao Kuang-hsiao 姚廣孝

Yen Ju-lüeh 艾儒略

Yishongna 伊桑阿

Yuan Dunasty 元朝

Yuan Shih 元史

Yung-lo 永樂

INDEX

219832 / Rood

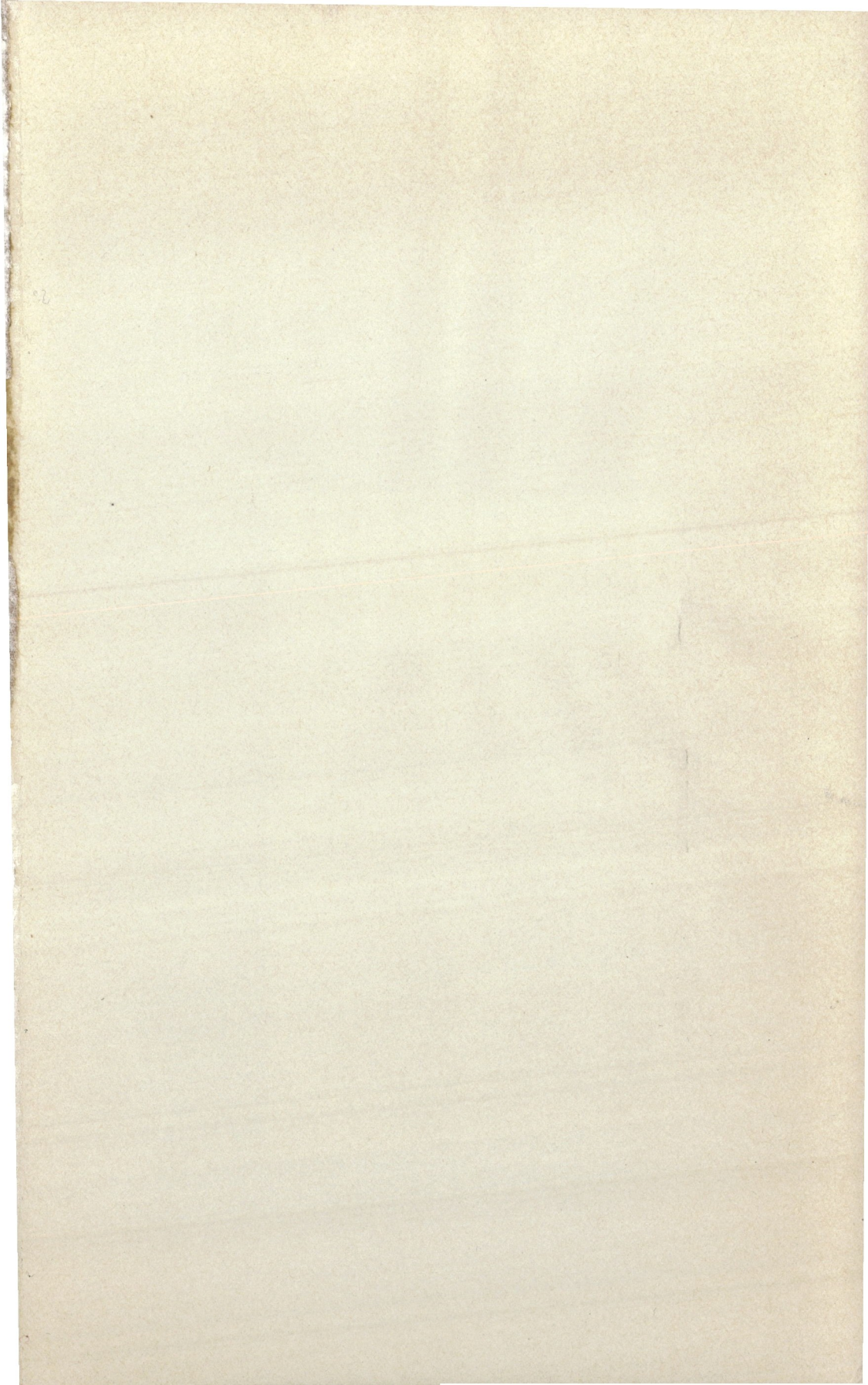

Soc
DS
740.5
R8
C47

DATE DUE

MAR 4 1974

MAY 1 2 1969 S.A.   MAY 1 2 1975

DEC 2 6 1977

OCT 2 3 1978

AUG 2 6 1969 S.A.   MAR 2 6 1979

DEC 1 6 2000   AUG 2 3 1975

NOV 1 1971 S.A.   APR 2 3 1999

FEB 1 1974   MAR 1 3 1974 S.A.